To Pam —

All the best to you!

Enjoy —

"Linda Lou"

XOXO

Bastard Husband

A Love Story

Linda Lou

Aging Nymphs Media LLC
Las Vegas, Nevada

For my dear friend

Nina

and courageous women everywhere
who've started over in life,

sometimes kicking and screaming

Acknowledgements

I am indebted to the members of the Henderson Writers' Group (www.hendersonwritersgroup.com), who endured my early drafts week after week and provided gentle feedback. Your critique and ongoing encouragement have been invaluable to me. Special thanks to Jo Wilkins (www.mysticpublishers.com) and Gregory A, Kompes (www.kompes.com) for so generously sharing your expertise.

I also wish to extend my gratitude to my fine editorial team— Gregory A. Kompes, Deb Wilborn, Carrie Lahain, Diane Weikert, Lisa McGlaun and Ketti Horton—for helping me craft this story.

Thank you to my many dear friends who graciously volunteered to be test readers and to my blogging buddies and blog readers around the world for urging me to share my story. Sincere thanks to the members of the Divorced and Widowed Adjustment Group, who were my first friends in Las Vegas.

My deepest gratitude goes to Mom, who's been my champion from day one, and to my sister Lori for her undying devotion.

Finally, for the abundance of gifts he brought to my life and for his insistence to walk his path alone, I thank my Kiwi ex.

Author's Note

This memoir is based on my experience over a one-year period beginning June 1, 2004. The events described are real, though by nature, a memoir reflects a representation of the truth as recounted through the filter of the author's own recollection. Some names have been changed, some characters were combined, and some events were compressed to facilitate the movement of the story.

PART I

1.

Today I put my bastard husband on a plane to the other side of the world. He wasn't always a bastard. He was perfect and I loved everything about him. Well, almost everything. I may never see him again.

There were no last hugs, not even a half-hearted effort to put a few words together. I could have easily come to a rolling stop at the airport and pushed his ass into the passenger drop-off lane; instead, I parked in the short-term lot and stayed with him throughout the check-in process, hoping, I suppose, to see some flicker of caring on his part. But we plodded through the terminal in silence, and when we reached the security checkpoint where I could go no further, he looked in my direction and said, "See ya."

See ya?

As he walked away and found his place in line, I gave him the finger, right there in the crowded airport. I do that a lot in public places, usually while trying to coax him off a barstool and away from a new-found friend with tavern wisdom far more compelling than anything I have to offer. Hell, I gave him the finger two nights ago in the Green Valley Ranch Casino when I couldn't pry him from the poker table before he marched off on his own because "the dealer gypped him." He is never aware of my gesture, and although it's not my most mature practice, I do enjoy an adolescent satisfaction in my passive-aggressive retaliation. It's just that it wouldn't have killed him to give me a proper good-bye.

See ya?

Now home from the airport, I furiously snatch random items—his Far Side coffee cup, shaving apparatus left in the bathtub, nice LL Bean slippers I'd given him one Christmas—and stuff them into an old duffel bag. He shipped out twenty-five boxes of his crap before we moved here, so there aren't too many reminders left. I don't want to see any evidence of his existence; my raging blood pressure is proof enough.

I toss the bag into the front closet and stand in the middle of the living room, chest heaving. The apartment looks nice. You'd never know we've been here only six days—pictures on the wall and everything. This was our third move in less than two years; we've gotten good at it. We've had a fair division of labor—each time he's set up the computer, TV, and anything involving wires or assembly of any kind while I put together the kitchen and bathroom. We had fun determining the best arrangement for the furniture and in no time the place looked like we'd lived in it forever.

I like it here. The vibe is comfortable and funky, with our Native American sand paintings, statues, candles, and rocks we've collected from our road trips throughout the West. From both the kitchen and the spare bedroom I can see the entire Las Vegas valley—Sunrise Mountain about ten miles straight ahead, the Strip thirteen miles to the northwest. Palm trees, sunshine…I feel like I'm on vacation, or on a business trip, living in a Marriott Residence Inn. At night there's an explosion of lights.

Glancing around the room, I enjoy a momentary sense of contentment. My eyes rest on a panoramic photo of the two of us on top of Medicine Bow Mountain outside Laramie, Wyoming. We stand smiling, arm in arm. I look thin and tan, which no doubt is why I display the picture, and he has a cute and happy expression. I've always loved his looks.

Not now, though. I scowl at his image, give him the finger, and return to my anger.

These past few days have sucked. I know he's been deliberately trying to piss me off, probably hoping he might press me to the point where I'd scream, *"Don't come back!"* Though the sentiment certainly bubbled—nearly erupted—no way would I give him such an easy out. He will never be able to say, "This is what you wanted. You told me not to come back."

I think of last Wednesday night when he left the apartment at about 11:30 to go out for cigarettes and then called at 9:30 the next morning from the Fiesta, a casino less than a mile up the road. He'd been playing poker all night.

"So how much did you win?" I asked, pretending to ignore the overwhelming odds that he didn't.

"About $200." So proud, he was. I later found ATM receipts revealing just how much it took to win that $200.

I said I'd come get him, and for a moment he seemed to consider my offer since the late May sun can be brutal here, especially, I imagine, if you've been up all night and are hung over as hell. He said he would walk home. Of course, he didn't say when.

At about 8:30 that evening I went to see if I could collect him. I walked through the casino, under the strings of multicolored lights, through the rows of ding-ding-dinging Lucky Sevens and Deuces Wild machines, and approached a lady in a purple vest behind one of the poker tables.

"By any chance, have you seen a chubby guy with an accent lately?" I asked.

Her sympathetic smile and the wisdom under her beehive hairdo said, Let me guess, he was only running down to the Speedy Mart for cigarettes.

"I know who you mean," she replied. Sure she does—bartenders and poker dealers always know who I mean. "I saw him not too long ago. He's probably still around somewhere."

Within minutes I found him at one of the bars, appearing surprisingly sober. His eyes looked tired, like my father's in the weeks before he died.

I couldn't get him to budge. Though his bar buddy was clearly full of shit, evidently the thought of going home was less appealing than listening to some drunken blowhard. I left alone, in familiar defeat.

A few hours later he finally trudged in, with that "I'm a grown man; I can stay out all night if I want" defiance that made me want to slap his face. He has yet to grasp the concept that when you're married there is another person in the equation.

I may never see him again. I am too angry to be sad.

§ § §

I wake up on my side of the bed. My first day alone in Las Vegas. No job, no friends, no bastard husband. I don't know exactly what to do today, but whatever it is, I don't feel like doing it. I'll lie here awhile longer. Whatever.

After a day of serious moping around and watching my entire daytime television lineup, I force myself to go pick up one of those arts and entertainment magazines you see in convenience stores. I need to find out what's going on around here; I have to do something.

Wow—does it really take only 15 minutes to walk to the Speedy Mart and back?

Scanning through the listings in the Meetings section, I decide to check out a divorce support group, listed between "Cross-Dressers of Las Vegas" and "Friends and Family of Incarcerated People." And I think *I* have problems.

The meeting is held in a preschool room of a Methodist church on West Flamingo and I am relieved to get there without a problem. I love to explore a new city, but hate trying to find everything. Typically I overshoot my destination and then have to make a U-turn, which usually prompts someone to lean on the horn or give me the finger. What goes around, comes around, right?

I take a seat in the circle and think I cannot believe I am sitting in a divorce support group.

I am sitting in a divorce support group.

Sometimes you catch yourself at different points in life and think, "I am doing *what*?" and you wonder how you got there, but when you piece it all together you realize there are simply no mysteries. And sometimes, like when you're in a plane 30,000 feet above the earth, it's best not to put too much thought into exactly where you are. This is one of those times.

The facilitator is a kind looking man named Chuck. Tattoos adorn each arm, not the intricate artwork I've seen on Harley riders, more like blurred reminders of bygone wartime service. He goes over the rules for the new people. That would be me.

"This meeting is a forum for sharing your emotions about the loss of a relationship," Chuck begins. "Everything you say is confidential, and we ask you don't repeat anything you hear outside this room. We rent the space here—we are not affiliated with the church."

Thank God.

Chuck continues. "This Tuesday night group is for people going through a divorce or separation from a significant relationship. The widowed group meets on Thursday nights."

Those lucky widows. Sorry, but I believe every woman who's unwillingly blown out the last candle of her marriage has wondered, "Wouldn't it be easier if he simply dropped dead?" Yes, anyone who says she'd rather explain the details of yet another failed marriage than bask in the sympathy of widowhood is a goddamn liar. Especially if you wanted to kill the bastard anyway, and believe me, I've been tempted.

I remember one night in Laramie, in our first house out West. He was stinkin' drunk and acting like such an asshole; the open door to the basement stairs downright teased me. All it would have taken was one good shove to send him flying into a heap on the concrete floor below.

That's not the kindest thought I've ever had. Especially about someone I love.

Chuck starts the meeting by asking each of us to rate our "emotional barometer" on a scale of one to ten, with one meaning you're in the shitter, and if you're a ten, you're on Cloud Nine (my words, not his). I say I am a five. Next, he calls on us randomly to "share."

A perfectly coiffed woman tells us her name is Mona and that she is newly separated after twenty-seven years of marriage. Her expression curdles at the mention of her husband's name. Another lady, also named Linda and who also has crappy hair, was married over thirty years to someone I don't think she liked too much, either. Still, this must suck for them to have their lives change so drastically after such a long time. It sucks for me and it's been only two and a half years. Most everyone here seems to be reacting to someone else's decision to leave the relationship; they're the ones who've been dumped, to put it less sensitively. I guess the ones who did the dumping are happily out there on their own, maybe with their new playmates. Or maybe they're on the other side of the world drinking themselves to death.

I half listen as each broken heart exposes itself; the other half of me prepares the monologue for when it's my turn. I should at least try to make it interesting. A petite woman with what looks to be a Toni home perm currently has the floor.

"Then the washing machine broke...I think it needed a new belt... or maybe it was the motor... and I had to call Tommy to come look at it...I didn't want to see him...but I had to wash my clothes..."

Time goes in reverse as she drones away and I am convinced she belongs in the Thursday night widows' group, for surely her husband died of boredom.

Chuck calls on me next. I notice the Absolutely No Swearing sign hanging from the ceiling. This will be a challenge.

I open with, "I'm Linda. I just moved to Las Vegas one week ago. I have no husband, no job, and you people are my only friends."

Everybody laughs at my pathetic truth.

"Yesterday my husband left for New Zealand, where he's from. Sorry, I still call him my husband, but we actually got divorced before we left Utah, where we lived for the past year. He still has his job there at the university; he's off for the summer. He doesn't know if he's coming back to the States or not. The only reason we got divorced was in case he doesn't.

"He's my second husband," I continue, "and...he's a drinker. I guess he's what you'd call a 'functioning alcoholic,' but he could be lured into any addictive behavior—gambling, cigarettes, eating. He's a 'fill-in-the-blank-aholic.'"

A few people laugh, some nod.

"Not a workaholic, though," I continue, with my own stupid chuckle. "What I mean is, he doesn't have to try. He's brilliant, really." *On paper*, I want to add—as the word "brilliant" leaves my lips

I remember the day he thought he was going blind in one eye. Yeah, the guy with the Ph.D. had lost a lens in his glasses. The thought makes me smile. "I still love him very much," I add.

That's enough for now.

The people in this circle are the only ones who know we're divorced; I haven't yet told my family and friends back home. I dread the task, though certainly I've let some details slip that would indicate things are not quite as rosy as I'd like them to believe. It's best to keep this to myself; the concern in their eyes would be unbearable, even over the telephone. No one wants to hear you've slept in a closet to hide from your husband's return from the pub, though sometimes that's the only way to get a good night's sleep.

My story to the outside world is that we moved to Las Vegas because the job opportunities would be better for me here. He'll continue to teach during the week in Utah, driving up on Monday mornings and staying in a cheap motel during the week. And in real life, that is our plan, if he does come back. It's probably not a good plan, since I can already tell Las Vegas is not the best place for a guy who can spend twenty-three straight hours in a casino. Or maybe it's the perfect place for someone like that, just lousy for his wife.

§ § §

There's a message on my voicemail when I get home. "Hi, Linda. I thought I would let you know I got here alright. Okay, then. Talk to you later." His tone is odd and formal—we never call each other by name, preferring terms of endearment such as "honey" and "babe." When he starts off with "Hi, Linda," he might as well be talking to a stranger. I bet his mother said, "Did you call Linda yet?" and so he called, out of obligation.

I don't have it in me to respond right now. His apathetic farewell at the airport is back in my brain, so he can fuck off.

2.

You have a big ass and your kids are brats. That's what I wanted to say to the woman in front of me at Walgreen's this morning.

He's been gone two weeks. I'm so depressed and miserable, even Jesus would cross the street if he saw me coming. So in a perverse attempt to see just how far I can press the despondency, here I am at the mall shopping for a bathing suit.

After sifting through the racks, I enter the dressing room with eight options in hand, holding particular hope for a cute little number with diamond-shaped cutouts strategically running down the sides. Between the hanger and my body, however, something goes horribly wrong and the thought that security personnel might be watching through a one-way mirror sends me into a panic. I'm not concerned about modesty; I would just hate to gross anyone out.

I decide on a simple black two-piece (not a bikini, for God's sake) that actually doesn't look too bad. I haven't worn anything but a maillot for the past twenty-five years, but I've seen what other women wear poolside at my apartment complex and I think I can get away with this.

The minute I get home, I try on my purchase again to make sure I didn't gain weight in transit and that the mirrors in the store didn't make me look dubiously thinner. I think sometimes they do.

I'm still safe. The bottom is cut high enough to hide most of the stretch marks on my stomach and the bra top makes my boobs look a little bigger than they actually are. I don't look bad. Hell, I look pretty good.

There's still about an hour until *Guiding Light* comes on, so I have time for a swim. This is my life: get up, meditate, do some yoga, read the paper and do both crosswords, give his picture the finger every time I walk by it, go to the pool, and then at two o'clock I watch my soap while eating two bowls of mocha almond fudge ice cream. I kind of like this routine, especially since at some point I'm going to have to get a job.

I wrap a mini-sarong around my waist, tighten my abs and strut myself down to the pool. As I approach the gate, I pass a woman about my mother's age and a little blond girl in a frilly pink bathing suit with matching flip-flops. I smile at them with the confidence that comes when you know you're looking good.

The woman smiles back and points to me. "Look, Emily!" she singsongs. "That lady looks like your other grandmother!"

Did she say I look like somebody's grandmother?

Well, I am, in fact, a grandmother, but I do NOT look like one. In good lighting, I can pass for thirty-nine, which is much too young to be a grandmother, even in Las Vegas.

Jesus Christ, lady, do you have any idea how fragile my self-esteem is? My dipsomaniac husband left ME because he needs to "return to his homeland" and I don't know if he's coming back or not, and if he doesn't, I'll have to start dating again and break in a new guy, in which case, the situation will eventually lead to nudity—maybe with the lights on—which quite honestly I wouldn't have worried about until you had to make that stupid fucking comment.

Glaring at the bitch, I say to little Emily, "Your other grandmother must be hot."

3.

I grew up in Albany, New York, where I lived for the first forty-three years of my life. I'm the oldest of five kids spaced over a fourteen-year period, which means I was in ninth grade when my little sister was born. My mother and the girl who sat next to me in French class were pregnant at the same time. Yuk.

Maybe because she always had a new baby to be home with, Mom became increasingly comfortable staying in the house, eventually to the point where she couldn't leave. She developed agoraphobia and was often doped up on "nerve pills," which kept her sacked out on the couch for most of the day, waking up for only two things: *Jeopardy* and the weather during the six o'clock news. Considering she never left the house, the obsession with the weather seemed a bit peculiar. Perhaps she wondered, "Will I need the heavy afghan over me tomorrow or just a light cotton blanket?"

My father, like his father, worked as a salesman for the Metropolitan Life Insurance Company, a job he hated but held until after his parents died. Once they were gone, he pursued a position more in line with his natural talent—he became a bus driver. Daddy loved driving the bus. "I don't work," he'd brag, "I drive other people to work." He'd sign up for all the overtime he could, no doubt to get out of the house since my mother never left it. Work was the one place Daddy could get some peace and quiet, and in an effort to reduce the passenger load, he'd sometimes ask the riders, "Have you ever thought of buying a car? Everyone has a car these days." They'd laugh at his good-natured ribbing, but I'm sure he would have dropped them off at the auto showroom had one been on his route.

So in our house, we had five kids, two parents, and one bathroom, where my father lived when he was home. He'd head upstairs with the paper, his coffee, the racing forms…strip down to his boxer shorts and T-shirt…and settle in. And if we had to pee before his next work shift, it was too goddamn bad. Good thing he wasn't around much, because by now we'd all be hooked up to dialysis machines. I remember no matter how desperately you had to go, you never wanted to be first in line once he finished up, for the ensuing stench was the most vile combination of shit and Old Spice you could possibly imagine. Daddy died four years ago, sitting on the toilet. Surely it was the law of averages.

As for me, I was a shy and quiet child, a bookworm with big dreams, mostly of escaping from the nuthouse. At age eight, I wrote a letter to whomever I thought was in charge of the TV show *Bonanza* suggesting they write in a part for a younger sister, to be played by me, of course. I offered some possible storylines and assured them that although I had never actually been on a horse, I was certainly willing to learn. In response, I received a colored glossy photo signed by all the Cartwright men, but alas, no offer of an acting contract.

A year later, I sent Johnny Carson a few of my favorite jokes, fantasizing about how the audience would roar when he opened his monologue with, "How did Captain Hook die?…He wiped himself with the wrong hand!" Fancying myself as quite mature for my age, and to address Johnny's older, late-night demographic, I also included what I thought was a solid demonstration of my ability to write adult humor: "What's pink and squishy and lies at the bottom of the ocean? Moby's Dick!"

Those were my first experiences with rejection, which even back then I regarded not as a reflection of my own shortcomings, but the result of someone else's regrettable lack of insight.

Once I hit high school I grew more outgoing and my studies became secondary to my social life. I was captain of the cheerleaders, vice president of my senior class, and my popularity continued into college, where I enjoyed the party culture of Plattsburgh State University, a school nestled in the tundra twenty miles from the Canadian border. I joined the campus radio station (I was one of the first female disc jockeys on the air), and earned my drinking money modeling for art classes, one of the many facts of campus life I conveniently withheld from my parents.

Things changed soon after the end of my freshman year. Gary Krisanda, one of my high school boyfriends, drowned Memorial Day weekend of 1976. His death marked the saddest point of my life. I needed answers: Why did this happen? Where is he now? I searched for explanations in books on the afterlife and psychic phenomena, something in which I had an interest going back to fifth grade. I remember waking up one Sunday morning with a feeling of unexplained certainty that one of my idols, Helen Keller, had died. The front page of the morning newspaper confirmed my premonition. The experience stayed with me, and my school term papers invariably involved ESP, the paranormal and the occult, which concerned my mother to the point that she'd stay awake long enough to review my compositions.

By the time the bicentennial came around, I had met Chris Blackwell, a cool-looking, laid-back musician type. I thought he was a gift from above to help me cope with my immeasurable grief over Gary's death. Chris and I were married in November 1977, and after a miraculous three-month pregnancy we had our first child, Christopher Jackson, named after singer-songwriter Jackson Browne. I remember calling my parents to say I'd started labor and was heading to the hospital. My father offered a tender bit of advice, words that remain with me to this day: "Good luck," he said, "and don't go home empty-handed." Twelve and a half months later Chris and I had a daughter, Courtney Lynne (named after nobody). I was twenty-one.

Starting a family that young means you begin your adult life in a financial hole. We struggled for years on end, dodging creditors and living paycheck-to-paycheck while I finished my undergraduate education and then grad school. But we set family vacations as a top priority, always finding the money to take the kids camping in the Adirondacks or sometimes we'd splurge for a motel room over in Hampton Beach. We'd pack up the Subaru, praying that whatever lurked behind the flashing "Service Engine Soon" light would hold off until we got back home. Oil changes were not in the budget.

Although we were supposed to be grown-ups, we continued to live like students, right down to hosting the periodic beer parties, complete with blasting music that sometimes prompted the Albany Police to pay us a visit per the request of a justifiably angry neighbor. The kids, about six and seven years old at the time, loved to play bartender, carefully filling our guests' plastic cups from the keg. Thrilled with the tips their patrons would offer, they eagerly promoted refills in total oblivion to the consequences of DWI legislation.

Our home décor consisted of posters of rock stars and treasures Chris would find on the curb on trash night. Nearly all our furniture came from relatives who had died or gone into nursing homes. We even bought our house (with the help of some very creative financing) from Chris's great aunt, who went off to live in an assisted living facility.

Maintaining an old colonial with a bathroom that should have been remodeled two generations before further strained our budget. Chris found a way to rig up a shower by running plastic tubing from the sink, a temporary fix that lasted about ten years. The old stove required pliers to turn the gas on and off, which mortified the kids as they got older and had friends over for dinner.

Our poor kids. Most of their classmates lived in houses that seemed, well . . . more adult. Their couches didn't need to be covered with Indian bedspreads. They had new patio furniture, while the rickety chairs on our front porch looked straight off the set of *Sanford and Son*. Yet despite the lack of material assets, the kids seemed thrilled with the parents they were born to, just as I was, as crazy as that may sound.

After eighteen years together—half my life—Chris and I split up. Seeking to understand my role in the failure of our marriage, I immersed myself in books by New Age thinkers such as Louise Hay and Deepak Chopra. My readings helped me gain perspective, and throughout the years, Chris and I have remained on friendly terms. Together we welcomed our precious grandson, Connor Burns, the day after Christmas 1998, with Courtney, at age nineteen, evidently continuing the family tradition of reproducing while the eggs are still fresh. And while I felt concern about her ability to handle the challenges of motherhood at such a young age, I trusted the divine order of the universe and knew everything was perfect.

I'm not so sure I trust the divine order of the universe right now.

4.

It's a beautiful sunny day in Las Vegas, just like yesterday was and just like tomorrow is sure to be. At 10 am, the temperature is already a hundred degrees, but the heat doesn't bother me. All I have to do is think of Albany in January.

This is the best I've felt since he's been gone. I like what I'm wearing—tan short shorts and a black Sonic Youth tank top—and I'm happy with my weight (126.5 before breakfast, down a pound from last week). I'm not only having a thin day, I'm having a good hair day and a good face day, too—the Triple Crown of confidence.

With the stars in alignment, it's an opportune time to get my new driver's license. I've been smiling in the mirror all morning, practicing for my picture. Smiling comes easy to me; except for lately, I'm generally quite cheerful. Sometimes I have to consciously tone down the buoyancy, like when I'm at a wake for someone I really don't know and forget I'm supposed to be sad. I smile even when I'm having a shitty day, at least in public, though I don't think I ever sit around the house frowning. I'm more of a scowler anyway.

This will be my third license in less than two years. A trip to the DMV is never a pleasant chore, but I don't mind. I'd rather sit amongst grumpy, smelly strangers than, say, look for a job. Not that I really want a job, though if he doesn't come back, I won't have a choice.

I've been lucky. Aside from teaching yoga and the occasional freelance writing gig, I haven't had to work since we moved out West, which has been fine with me. I did, however, work part-time when we lived in Utah; one of my yoga students was a physician and for a few months I helped out in his office. Dr. Turner was an actual doctor, with a diploma and everything, except he practiced medicine using his psychic abilities. He'd stand next to the patient, close his eyes and would pull on his index finger until the diagnosis came to him from... I don't know where . . . and then he'd send them off to buy natural remedies from the herb shop next door. Everyone loved Dr. Turner, and patients came from all over to see him. He closed his practice shortly after a couple of men in business suits showed up and started snooping around the office. Too bad.

Other than casino jobs, I haven't seen a thing in the Sunday paper, but I have responded to a few postings on Monster. That's about the extent of my effort. I've been in no mood to cold-call prospective employers, and even though I'm feeling quite sure of myself today, I'm not about to waste my Triple Crown spirits on job search activities.

The DMV is a madhouse, as I expected. Something like six thousand people move to Las Vegas every month, and we all need a Nevada license. I take my place in line to get a number that will lead to another wait. Whatever. As long as I'm home before *Guiding Light*, I don't care. I think I'll say my weight is 125, which it would have been if I hadn't had those two bowls of ice cream before bed last night.

The guy ahead of me is a pleasant looking character who could pass for Jerry Garcia's younger brother. You don't see any hippies in Las Vegas, I've noticed. His head is a frenzy of dark curls and although we're in a windowless tomb of bureaucracy, he's wearing sunglasses. I wonder why such a young person would need a cane.

He grins radiantly at me, as if he's holding a winning jackpot ticket and this is the line to cash it in. Or maybe he appreciates my cute outfit. I smile back.

"Sonic Youth," he comments, noticing my shirt. "I've never been to one of their shows."

"Oh, I've been to, like, six or seven," I say, "back in New York." Yeah, I'm cool. I don't mention I saw them with my son and his friends.

The clerk gives us our numbers and license applications. We find two empty seats together, and within minutes I know all about my new friend. His name is Dan and he's forty-one, four years younger than me. He writes concert reviews for some music website I've never heard of. Turns out he grew up on Long Island and spent a few years upstate around the Albany area. As we fill out our paperwork, we reminisce about the old JB Scott's nightclub on Central Avenue and the concerts we saw at the Saratoga Performing Arts Center for only five bucks. Dan's wife lives in Phoenix, but he doesn't say why. I'm glad he has a wife.

Dan spits when he talks, but nothing lands on me, so I don't care. I hang onto his every word. Other than the people in the divorce support group, my social life so far has consisted of small talk with bank tellers, grocery store clerks, and Starbucks baristas, and they always have to move on to the next customer. I even offered to make the cable guy a sandwich so he'd stay awhile after he hooked me up. Right now I'm thrilled to be having a conversation.

Dan's number summons him to a window and with the cane, he gets there when he gets there. Soon it's my turn with another attendant. I smile (of course) as I hand my Utah license and my neatly prepared application to a woman whose name tag says "Diane." She's probably a little younger than me, but her face suggests a harder life.

"Diane—that's my mother's name," I comment, as if she gives a shit.

But she does. "Really?" Her face brightens. "Linda is my sister's name."

"We're practically related!" I'm developing quite the repertoire of idiotic chitchat to lay on counter personnel.

Diane defies the stereotype of the DMV customer service shrew. She handles my transaction with congenial efficiency and then directs me to stand on the gray line taped to the floor.

"Smile, honey," she says.

I love it when waitresses and other service people call me honey, especially these days. I smile, and I mean it.

Dan's waited for me, and together we make our way through the crowd toward the front door, emanating an ever-so-slight sense of superiority over the poor chumps who still have a long wait ahead of them.

"I'm parked way at the end of the lot," I say.

"Me, too!" Dan is one happy hippie.

As we head down a row of cars, I wonder why he didn't park up front in a handicapped spot. "So what's with the cane?" I ask, noting that two weeks of solitude have begun to erode my social skills.

"Cerebral palsy. Just on my left side." He beams as if I should be jealous.

It's so good to stroll alongside someone, I'm not even annoyed that I have to walk so slowly because of his condition. Yikes, he never shuts up, but who do I have to listen to these days? I like that he's doing all the talking; Dan's chatter saves me from disclosing my own drama. We discover our cars are parked right next to each other, and stop and smile at each other in awe of synchronicity.

He's still yakity-yakking about the ninety-seven times he's seen the Grateful Dead, even after I open my car door and slide in. We finally say good-bye and see you at a show sometime, and I think how important it is to be your nice self, like Dan and Diane, when you talk to people you don't know. You can really make somebody's day, and it may be the best one they've had in a while.

Today's a good day.

5.

Here in Las Vegas, I am no one's wife, mother, sister, daughter, co-worker, friend, or lover. I have no one to accommodate; I have no roles to play. I am just myself, by myself.

I'm okay being alone, probably because before we moved out West I spent lots of time traveling for business. In my old life I worked as a corporate trainer, technical writer, or a combination of the two, but always as an independent contractor working from project to project. That arrangement allowed me to live on the periphery of the workplace dynamics and therefore avoid all the bullshit that comes with office politics, which was fine with me.

Wearing a business suit makes me feel like a kid playing dress-up. *Here I am at work! Trick or Treat!* In defiance of the corporate dress code, I used to shorten my skirts to the point where one more millimeter would have really pushed the envelope. Yes, I prefer the fun-loving, "sexy, yet professional" look over the dour image many women in business suits project.

Like most people, I've never enjoyed working, except I readily admit it. Work is a way to make money so I can have fun in real life. I've never tied my sense of self-worth to my career, and have gotten away with this piss-poor attitude only because I'm very good at what I do.

I knew work would be a part of life that was going to suck as soon as I started my first job back in 1971 at the dry cleaners down the street from my house on Lincoln Avenue. In one hundred ten-degree heat from the machines, I tagged and prepared garments, which often involved the revolting task of pulling dirty Kleenex out of old guys' pants pockets.

Of the three brothers who owned the business, Irving Freedman was the oldest, and in my fourteen-year-old opinion, the most entertaining. A tiny man with huge glasses that sat on his face like black-rimmed windowpanes, his only apparent function was to unnerve his brothers, Morty and Charlie. I liked Irv, not just because he rattled Morty to the point where the poor guy developed a noticeable tic, but because he never talked to me as if I were just a kid. One day, puffing on his omnipresent cigar, Irving looked at me and declared with quiet resignation, "You know, Tootsie... it's all Nixon's fault." Whatever that meant, I nodded with wide-eyed allegiance, appreciating his sharing of such profound insight.

My life on the road began in 1997 with a gig at General Electric's world headquarters in Fairfield, Connecticut, the epicenter of the soulless corporate universe. I was part of a team of instructional designers tasked with documenting GE's Six Sigma quality initiative, a topic I truly could not give a shit about then or now.

My job involved endless consultation with "subject matter experts," extremely bright and career-focused engineer-types intent on proving their status as "A players" in the GE culture. Tied to their voicemail and email even on weekends and during vacations, they were forever expected to do more, faster. A sad existence, I thought. While the geniuses bickered about some aspect of process control, I dreamed of a dive bar I might visit after work where I could shoot pool and drink Guinness with regular guys in flannel shirts, who despite their pedestrian IQs, at least made it to their kids' soccer games.

My status as a contractor allowed me to take liberties not extended to career employees who fretted over their position on the corporate ladder. Instead of posting flow charts and project timetables, I decorated my work cubicle with healing crystals, Mardi-Gras beads, and Pee Wee Herman memorabilia. My coworkers often hung out in my cube, a refuge from the drudgery, and a few of us bonded immediately after discovering we shared an unusually high tolerance for politically incorrect and sexually explicit humor.

The work was dreadful, meaningless, and the project was ultimately shelved, but I welcomed the income and I realized sometimes it doesn't matter what you do—sometimes you're not there for the work at all. I was there to make those friends. Like old Irv Freedman, they were the bright spot in a dismal existence.

For the two-year duration of the project, GE put me up in the hotel of my choice, all expenses paid. I drove down from Albany to Connecticut on Monday mornings, listening to Howard Stern the whole way, and returned home Friday evenings. I didn't mind being away. By then Chris and I had been split up for a few years, the kids were on their own, and I was happy to get out of town. Besides, I liked hotel life—I didn't have to cook or clean, and after work I had the whole evening to myself.

After the GE job, I got another gig that again required constant travel, this time throughout the Northeast. Not one to spend night after night eating room service in front of the TV, I'd explore the local area, find a yoga class to take, or check out the hotel lounge. Initially I found the scene a bit depressing, full of middle-aged businessmen indistinguishable from each other, marking time until the next day when they could go back to work or fly home. But eventually I learned lounge talk could be fun.

Inevitably I'd be the only female sitting at the bar. Usually I mulled over a piece of work-related writing that wasn't quite coming together and perhaps needed some alcohol-induced insight. Within minutes, one of the suits would approach me with the predictable interrogation: "What are you working on?" "Where are you from?" and the dreaded, "What do you do for a living?"

I'm a technical writer on contract to develop an online performance support system. God help me, I bored even myself with that answer. Usually the suit had an equally incomprehensible job that I wouldn't bother to try to understand. I had to make things interesting.

I'm an actress on As the World Turns. I liked that one. Then I'd sermonize on how daytime dramas are a misunderstood medium and should be duly recognized for their contribution to American pop culture. *"Guiding Light*'s been on the air for over 50 years," I'd tell them. "It's in the *Guinness Book of World Records*, you know." If that didn't scare them away, I might lean a bit closer, look them intently in the eye, and ask, "And what do *you* want to be when you grow up?"

I came to enjoy what I called "social bungee jumping," taking risks and exploring uncharted territories of human interaction, however superficial. The last thing I wanted to talk about was work, but I soaked it in when someone shared the details of his personal life. I listened empathetically to their stories of a wife's struggle with breast cancer and the teenage son who may be hiding a drug problem. Everyone's life is interesting, especially when people trust you enough to tell you the juicy parts. I think it's easier to tell your tale to strangers you'll never see again.

§ § §

One night in the Marriott lounge outside of Buffalo, a pleasant-looking Indian man sitting next to me asked, "Are you writing about all the characters you see in here?"

"I wish." I smiled, folding my papers. "This is work crap."

"You'll like my friend here," he said, pointing to the casually-dressed fellow next to him who looked like he'd done some time on a rugby field. "The two of you should talk."

The rugby guy seemed like the playful type. "Light beer?" I teased with mock distain as I held up my Guinness. "You don't know how to drink!" I'd be eating those words in time.

I eyed his cigarette. "Does this bother you?" he asked, waving his hand around me.

"Oh, no. You're fine." *Lie.* I can't stand sitting in smoke, but he sounded like he was from England, and I'm shallow enough that I can overlook a lot for a cool-sounding accent.

"So what do you do?" I asked, downright ashamed of myself for stooping to pose the question I hated the most.

He motioned toward his buddy. "We're taxi drivers."

"That's a relief. I was afraid you were going to say 'systems analyst' or 'field engineer.'" He's cute, I thought. "So what's it like to be a cab driver? Are people nice?"

He suppressed a laugh before coming clean. "We're professors at the university. We're here tonight with some students for our end-of-semester celebration." Clearly thrilled that he could pass for a hack, he wanted confirmation. "You believed me, eh?"

"Eh? You from Canada?" I asked.

"New Zealand. Australia's Canada. I've been here twelve years, eh."

I picked up that "eh" could be tacked on to the end of a statement, as well as a question.

He told me he grew up on a farm in New Zealand and lived in Australia and England before coming to the U.S. After a while the conversation somehow turned to our fathers. His died many years before at the age of fifty-two, mine had been gone for little more than a year. I liked talking about them and found it comforting to be with someone who understood the loss. His smile and the twinkle in his blue eyes gave me the impression my new friend was having the most enjoyable conversation ever, even though the subject was our poor, dead dads.

Before we parted, we made plans to go out the following Tuesday night when I'd be back in town. Normally that would translate to a week of first-date preparation anxiety, but I approached our rendez-vous with pleasant anticipation. I didn't feel I had to pray for a good hair day or try on every outfit I owned to see which one made me look the thinnest. Everything was different; the old rules no longer applied. When the big evening arrived and he picked me up in the Marriott lobby, I felt so at ease, my neck didn't even blotch up.

Sitting in his Chevy Nova, I was impressed that someone with such a good job would drive such a piece of crap. Like many women, I believe the hotter the car, the smaller the anatomy. He must be huge, I thought. I checked him out as he drove. Having seen him only once in a dark lounge, I wanted to get a better look.

Most people find true love when they gaze into a person's eyes, but the nose did it for me. His little ski-jump model seemed a bit delicate for his beefy physique, and it struck me as the cutest thing I'd ever seen.

I noticed his choice of white socks with brown shoes. Not every man has to be Calvin Klein.

I noticed a sizable belly hanging over his belt. Great, I thought, I don't have to hold in *my* gut all night.

I noticed the fabric drooping from the roof of the car. *Caught!*

"I tacked that up today," my date said, feigning pride. "I wanted to make a good impression."

"Thank you! I feel so important!" I gushed. I loved him at that moment.

We had a typical first-date agenda for the evening—lots of talking over drinks and dinner. "It's funny that you're from Albany," he said, as the waiter walked away with his Visa card.

"Why is that?"

"My dad liked to quiz people about the U.S. state capitals. His favorite question was, 'What is the capital of New York?' In New Zealand everyone thinks it's New York City, eh. Dad would have loved you. You're so American."

I had no idea what that meant and didn't bother to ask. I was too busy wondering if people in the restaurant could see the hearts shooting out of me, like the love-struck characters in cartoons.

"How far is Albany from Saratoga?" he asked.

"Albany's about a half-hour south."

"Have you been to the horse races?"

"Sure. My father brought me and my sister to the harness track as often as my mother would let him. When his horse came in, he'd yell, 'Come on, girls!' so everyone around us knew he was a winner, and we'd skip after him to the betting window."

I liked sharing the memory and my date appreciated my story. "I used to go to the trots with my dad, too," he said. "So we were both at the races with our dads, on opposite sides of the world."

"But at different times," I added. "Let's see, when I was eight years old, you were…"

"Not born yet!" he laughed.

"Thanks for reminding me."

"I miss my dad," he said.

"Yeah, I miss mine, too." We studied each other's faces a while. "I booked a room on the Canadian side of Niagara Falls for next weekend. The company I work for is putting me up since I have to be here in Buffalo for the next two weeks."

I took the last sip of decaf and asked a question I already knew the answer to. "Would you like to join me?"

§ § §

I stood at my hotel room window directly overlooking Horseshoe Falls, the anticipation of his arrival overshadowing nature's magnificence. I'd met him only eight days before, yet I knew I stood on the edge of something as powerful as the Falls below.

At last I heard the knock I'd been waiting for. I opened the door and as we hugged I felt our energies blend with the force of a hundred bolts of lightning.

"Shall we check out the pub downstairs?" he asked when we released the embrace.

"Sure." Waving the remote, I clicked off the TV. "I want you to know, I just did something I never thought I'd ever, ever do for a man." I paused for dramatic effect. "I just turned off the Daytime Emmy Awards. You must understand the significance—the Daytime Emmys are my Super Bowl Sunday."

"Is that so?" he said, without a trace of judgment. I offered more as we headed for the elevator.

"Every year my sisters and I buy a couple of six packs and we make dips and stuff, just like Super Bowl people. Except we light candles when our *Guiding Light* stars win." I searched for a reaction, but still nothing. "Pretty queer, huh?"

The elevator doors opened and we stepped in. He grinned, unfazed. "Everyone has something they fancy."

We settled on two stools at the end of the bar, where we laughed and drank and sang Happy Birthday to someone and drank and laughed until last call. I signed our ninety-four dollar bar tab to my corporate account without the slightest hint of guilt and then we headed back up to the room.

As drunk as we both must have been, our first venture into physical connection proved mutually satisfying. "I like your body," I told him as my fingers played across his chest.

"I like your body, too. You feel so tiny."

You feel so tiny. Men have no idea of the magical powers of those simple words. If they only knew how easily they'd get laid by speaking them. We explored each other, as first-time lovers do, explaining scars and pointing out moles.

"Don't I have the worst stretch marks you've ever seen?" I asked as his hands slid over my belly. Ordinarily I wouldn't call attention to what I'm sure is my least attractive body part, but I intuited his unconditional acceptance. "Love scars from babies."

"I think we should try to have one," he said. "We would have an amazing kid."

I contemplated the idea of procreating with someone I'd seen only three times, with no consideration of how absurd it might look in the light of day. "My kids are grown. I don't know if I could go back to that. They're a lot of work."

"Don't worry, honey, we'll put it in boarding school," he assured me.

"Oh, okay, then!" I playfully rolled on top of him and we started in again. The lone condom on the floor was the only one we'd ever use.

We barely slept all night. The intensity between us, the striking sense of fate, kept nudging us into awareness and we awakened now and then to share a thought or another tidbit of our lives.

"When I die, yours will be the last face I see," he said after one scattered moment of slumber.

I looked into his eyes.

He had more to share. "I remember the last time I saw my father. He shook my hand before I left New Zealand, and I knew at that moment I'd never see him again. I loved my father more than anyone in the world. I feel like weeping when I realize you'll never meet him. He would have been so proud that I'm with such a sweet woman."

"We have a lot to look forward to," I whispered.

We got up the next afternoon, ate breakfast, which I guess by then was lunch, then walked into town, where we stumbled upon the Casino Niagara and found a cozy sofa tucked away in the corner of an upstairs lounge. Still giddy from the night before, we sat as close to each other as we possibly could. "We're on our honeymoon!" he told our waitress as she set two Bloody Marys on the cocktail table in front of us. Whether or not she believed us, we toasted our counterfeit union with a "Cheers!"

"Here, let me show you something," I said, pulling a scribbled paper from my purse. "I had my tarot cards read a couple of months ago. Look, she said I would meet someone in three months, and I met you three months later, to the day."

He read through my notes. "The date in the corner, that's the date of your reading?"

I nodded.

"February 13. That's my birthday, eh. It's a sign," he said, with a certainty that all the planets had aligned specifically to create our experience.

Two drinks later, I got up to pee, touching his knee to steady myself as I rose. I opened the ladies' room door to find an attractive, well-dressed elderly woman lying on the floor.

"Can I help you?" I asked. Having been a hospice volunteer for several years, I was used to dealing with people in all sorts of discomforting predicaments.

"Please find my son," the woman pleaded.

"Certainly. I'll have him paged. What's his name?"

"His name is Michael McNeil."

"I'll be right back," I assured her.

I rushed to my beloved on the couch back in the lounge. "Go find security and have them page Michael McNeil. There's a lady on the floor in the bathroom. I have to get back to her."

"Will do," he said.

I went back to the woman, who now sat on the toilet in a stall, with the door open. "They're paging your son," I told her. Within minutes, the paramedics and Michael McNeil arrived. The woman thanked me for my help and I returned to my phony groom, who stood there in inexplicable red-faced exuberance.

"Babe! Michael McNeil! That's my father's name. Oh, my God— it's a sign! Will you marry me?"

"Of course." There could be no other possible answer. After all, I'd known him over a week and we were, after all, trying to conceive.

"I told you my father would love you. It's a sign! He's here with us right now."

"Could be. That's the only way for dead people to reach us— through signs," I reasoned. "It's not like they can come back to life and tap you on the shoulder."

We hung out a while longer, processing the experience and basking in the cosmic energy of the moment until I realized I still had a mission. The paramedics continued to work on poor Mrs. McNeil in the ladies' room off the lounge, so we decided to head back to our hotel room and I could use a bathroom on the casino floor on the way out. After taking the pee of my life, I returned to him in a second state of jubilation.

"Look, babe," he said, holding a plastic cup of quarters. "I played the machine while I was waiting for you. Look, I won! It's a sign!"

The previous night's ninety-four dollar bar tab was a sign, too. I didn't notice that one.

§ § §

Five months later, one night in late October, we lay in bed at his apartment in Buffalo. Out of nowhere, he asked me to marry him again, a more subdued proposal than the first: "What do you think, babe? It's time, eh?"

"Yes. It's time," I agreed, though just a few pages had been ripped off the calendar since we'd met. "Something low-key. No stress."

"Definitely."

"Let's go somewhere, just the two of us," I suggested. "It wouldn't be fair to get married in front of all of my family and not yours."

We talked about having a small wedding during his winter semester break in the New Age sanctuary of Sedona, Arizona, a fitting place for us, given our propensity for all things cosmic. It would be perfect.

The next morning I noticed none of the usual physical symptoms I'd been expecting for that time of the month, but I waited through the day before mentioning anything. "I'm supposed to get my period tomorrow, but my boobs don't feel achy. They usually feel tender right before my period," I told him after dinner.

"Something different, eh?" He smiled mischievously. "Maybe you're pregnant."

As if reading tea leaves, I looked for guidance in the pork chop bone on my plate, which suddenly nauseated me. "I don't know."

"Maybe we should pick up a test." He sprung up to clear the table, a job I normally took on.

"I'll get the dishes, honey. Sit down," I told him, making no effort to move.

"No, babe. You sit."

"Maybe you're right. I'll go get a test. I'll be right back."

During the half-block walk to Walgreens, I tried to wrap my head around the reality of the situation, though certainly this was not an occurrence left to chance. Pregnancy had been our goal since our first night together in Niagara Falls, and in the few months since then we carefully counted the days of my cycle to be sure we got in lots of sex when conditions seemed most favorable. Since he had the summer off, he often drove or flew to wherever I was working so we could be together. Once we spent an entire weekend in bed, choosing intimacy over the sunny days one holds so dearly in the Northeast. I ended up with a serious urinary tract infection from all the activity and had to spend two more days in bed, that time just lying there alone.

I scanned the selection of products in the feminine hygiene aisle. *Is it okay to buy the cheapest one?* It had been over twenty-two years since I last suspected I was pregnant, and back then there were no over-the-counter tests to perform in the secrecy of your bathroom, much less with immediate results. I remembered how, in college, I schlepped a jar of my first morning urine to the local Planned Parenthood and waited an agonizing day and a half for a counselor to call with the outcome. At least this pregnancy was planned.

I handed the box to the cashier, a woman about my age, and although she scanned the item without a hint of judgment, or any brain activity, I felt like a teenager making an illicit purchase. All kinds of thoughts shot through my brain during the short walk home.

Let's see, I just turned forty-three, so that means I'll still be forty-three by the time it's born—that's good. Not too ancient. And the kid's father will be, what? Thirty-five. Well, at least it'll have one parent who won't need bifocals to see it. That's good. October, November,

December...I'll be showing by the time we get married. Dammit! Just once I'd like to get married and not be pregnant. Oh, well...So my kids will be, what? Twenty-two and twenty-three, and Connor will be two. A pregnant grandmother...super. I wonder if you can dye your hair when you're pregnant. I hope so...Fuck it...I'm dying it anyway. I will not be a new mother with gray roots.

"I got it!" I announced upon my return, my cheeks bright red despite the mild autumn weather. He took the bag from me and pored over the instructions.

"Two lines you're pregnant, one line you're not. We'll know in five minutes."

I peed in the cup, dipped the little stick in the urine and carefully set it on the edge of the tub, thinking I probably should have sanitized the bathroom a bit first. My task completed, I sat next to him on the couch. We didn't say much, each of us lost in contemplation. Perhaps the prospect of first-time fatherhood consumed his thoughts, but as I stared into the coffee table, I could only think, when we get a place together, that Green Bay Packers candle *has* to go.

"It's time!" he said with the urgency of Christmas morning. "C'mon! Let's have a look."

I got up to follow him, and by the time I stepped into the bathroom, he'd already read the results. He turned and hugged me tightly.

"You're pregnant, babe."

6.

Lying poolside, I'm in no mood for the high-minded paperback, *Loving From Your Soul*, I stuck in my bag along with my towel and sunscreen. I got an email today. He wants to know if his *Economist* and *Investors Business Daily* are still coming.

I pretend to be absorbed in my book, but spend more time watching a man play in the water with his baby. I've seen him with his wife and little girl many times before; their apartment is directly across the parking lot from mine. They look nice and happy, but not in an annoying way. I've exchanged hellos with his wife, but have never spoken to him.

From my lounge chair, I can hear him talk sweetly to his baby. I'm sure he'd be an attentive daddy even if no one were watching. Occasionally he takes a juice box from the side of the pool and guides the straw to her mouth. Occasionally he guides a bottle of Heineken to his own mouth. It is 10:30 am. We're not in Utah anymore—this is Vegas, baby.

I read the words in my book with no comprehension, and instead think of how I could be playing with my own two-year-old. I turn the page, only because it's time.

§ § §

I don't recall what specifically prompted the impression, but I do remember sitting on the toilet in the middle of the night thinking, man, he can be a dick when he's drunk. I'd never seen him like that. Because of the pregnancy, I'd stopped drinking myself, and now viewed him through the unfiltered light of sobriety.

"So you were Mr. Asshole last night," I commented the next morning before we rose for the day.

"Yeah…I'm sorry," he said, cuddling up to me, seemingly sincere. "But please, honey, I worked hard for that Ph.D. It's *Dr.* Asshole." With that, he cracked himself up. I almost laughed, too, but something stabbed my gut.

"Oooh. I'm getting wicked cramps." I closed my eyes and breathed with conscious determination. He got up and returned with a glass of water, an act that reminded me of how I'd done the same for my mother when she'd cry after fighting with my father. I took a sip, and he stroked my clammy forehead, watching me with the same look I imagine I had as a child—hoping the water would have magical healing powers to make everything all right.

"Are you okay, babe?" he asked in the gentlest voice he owned.

"I don't know. I guess." Long, deep breaths. "It's probably just gas or something." The pain consumed me, but I enjoyed his tenderness, and after a few minutes, I started feeling better. No, better than better—horny. The nice version of him turned me on, and soon we started in on the very activity that got me in that situation in the first place.

§ § §

We looked forward to November 30, my first prenatal appointment. I lay on the table in the darkened room, and together we watched the ultrasound technician scrutinize the blotches on the screen. "Your last period was when?" she wanted to know.

"October 7," I replied. "The due date is July 13."

"Linda," she said, "it appears that the pregnancy is growing in the tube."

I knew what that meant, and it wasn't good. "It's ectopic?"

"It appears to be." Her eyes remained fixed on the machine, which saved her from having to look at either of us. "I'll go get the doctor," she said.

I waited for her to leave the room before bursting into tears. "No, no! It's a mistake!" I sobbed, as the father-to-be stared at the indecipherable image in silence.

Dr. Clark came in and confirmed the technician's diagnosis. "I'm going to admit you tonight and we'll do the surgery in the morning. I'll try to save the tube."

"Can you try to save the pregnancy?" I asked. *Get on the Internet now,* I wanted to tell him, *maybe there's been a miraculous breakthrough you don't know about yet.*

"No, I'm afraid I can't." In spite of his detached demeanor, I liked Dr. Clark. And I trusted him, having been under his scalpel the year before when he removed a large uterine fibroid. He was my second opinion for that surgery—the first doctor told me I needed a hysterectomy and not a physician in town could slice away only the tumor. She even sent me a letter to that effect, with the warning that if I couldn't abide by her proposed plan of treatment, she'd have no recourse but to drop me as a patient. Bitch. Never trust a female gynecologist with a moustache.

On our way out we stopped at the front desk to consult with Gloria, who took care of the hospital admission arrangements. Gloria projected that well-meaning, but unsettling niceness that people like funeral directors have—they wish they could feel sorry for you, but it's all in a day's work.

We stopped home to pack an overnight bag before heading for the hospital, the same hospital where I had the fibroid surgery. The scene was a depressing déjà vu—the paperwork, the request for a private room, the insistence on an epidural over general anesthesia. (I'm not above telling doctors how to do their jobs; I could tell the pope how to say Mass.) Yet I felt thankful for the familiarity; I would have wigged out had the experience been entirely new to me. In that context, I could understand why everything happens for a reason, but the reason behind losing the pregnancy eluded me. The next morning as the kind medical personnel wheeled me into the operating room, I wept until I lost consciousness. And so, I would not be a pregnant bride after all.

I woke up in recovery swathed in warm towels, happy to see his loving face. The surgery went well, he told me. The tube had to be taken, but it would not be impossible to get pregnant again. Dr. Clark said we could start trying in a month or so.

Still, I found no comfort in his promising prognosis. The previous year, I spent two post-surgical days walking the halls, making friends with the other patients and showing off my resiliency to the nursing staff. This time I stayed in my room and sulked until the discharge papers arrived.

With the pregnancy behind us, we focused on our wedding, which we planned for the end of the month, a few days after Christmas. We applied for a marriage license over the Internet and found a metaphysical minister, also through the Internet, who agreed to marry us at four o'clock on the balcony of the hotel we picked out overlooking Sedona's crimson sandstone towers. The apprehension I'd felt sitting on the john a few weeks before had dissipated, replaced by sorrow over losing the pregnancy and gratitude for his support.

The morning of our nuptials we hiked through red rocks and afterward relaxed in the hot tub, sharing our intentions with a biker couple from Ohio who offered to be our wedding photographers. Now *this* is the way to get married, we bragged—no hassles, no stress.

When it came time to get ready for the ceremony, I showered and did my make-up and hair the way I always do; no need to make a fuss. I unzipped the blue plastic garment bag I had ever-so-carefully protected during our flight, and oblivious to the possibility there could be more than one blue plastic garment bag in my closet at home, took out… my daughter's junior prom gown. As my fingers slid across Courtney's navy satin dress, which would have been tasteful enough to wear for the occasion, I lamented more than ever that I wasn't still a size 3. Fortunately, I didn't have to get married in hiking gear; I'd packed a separate bag with a little cocktail dress, in case we went out for New Year's Eve.

And so, the bride wore black. Another sign.

§ § §

I'm starting to roast in the July sun, so I sit on the bottom step of the pool, immersed up to my neck.

"Hi!" the man with the baby calls to me.

"Hi! Another hot one today." *Duh.* I really have to work on my small talk.

He wades toward me. "I'm Ari. This is Lauren," he says, stroking the little girl's hair.

"She's beautiful. How old is she?"

"She just turned two."

"I see she likes the water."

What would life be like with a two-year-old? Obviously he didn't stop drinking for me, but would he have stopped drinking for a child? Would we have been like those happy couples we sometimes passed on hiking trails with their precious little one nestled in a backpack? Or would we be in the midst of a nasty custody battle straddled between two hemispheres?

Thy will, not my will, I've learned. It's best that way—I don't know what the hell I want, and whatever I think I want never seems to be in my own best interest.

Ari and I talk while admiring little Lauren's every move. I'm pleased to be around her. Unlike in Utah, where little brats swarmed all over the place, I haven't seen many children here in Vegas.

He tells me he's from Israel and that he and his wife have lived in our apartment complex for three years.

"What does your husband do?" he asks, though I've not mentioned any husband.

"He's a professor," I answer, as if I actually have one. "He's away for the summer visiting his family in New Zealand." I don't tell him I may never see the prick again. It's been a nice morning.

"Let me know if you need anything," Ari says. "Everyone in Israel is neighborly, we help each other out. People aren't like that here. I mean it—just come over if we can ever help you."

I smile. His kindness makes my eyes well behind my sunglasses. "Thanks, I appreciate that." I need lots of help, Ari. You wouldn't know where to begin.

7.

Though she wasn't particularly religious, when I was growing up, my mother for some reason started nearly every sentence with *"JESUS CHRIST!"* And like all mothers, when she was really mad she would yell his full name, as listed on his birth certificate, which evidently is *"JESUS CHRIST ALL-GODDAMN MIGHTY!"* So in our house there was no associating Jesus with the all-loving, all-forgiving being worshipped around the world. No, the sound of his name was generally a prelude to an ass kicking.

It's a miracle I can even think about walking into a church since the words "Jesus Christ" should trigger some type of post-traumatic stress reaction, but it's Sunday morning and I'm trying out a "holistic" place I saw advertised in yesterday's newspaper.

Like many people, I end up in church only when someone gets married or dies and that's where they're holding the festivities. This is the first time I'm attending on a Sunday morning without being forced, which surely is a reflection of my current depressed mental state. Plus, I might meet some cool people at a metaphysical-type of church, so what the hell.

I turn off East Sahara into a strip mall housing a bizarre collection of storefronts. There's the Japanese Community Church, some crazy-looking type of Super-Jesus church, the Wig Outlet, and a nightclub offering Korean karaoke. I spot my destination—the University Church Institute.

I am going to a church next door to the Firearms Training Academy.

I'm a little early; I have to allow plenty of driving time in case I get lost. The man at the door smiles and hands me a program. I'm relieved no other church people rush over to welcome me. I take a seat in the back and think how I hated going to church as a kid. Every Sunday, my sister Lori and I were sentenced to the 10 a.m. service at Calvary Methodist Church with our father's parents, Nana and Papa.

No doubt my mother was psyched to get rid of us for a couple of hours, leaving her home with the younger kids, who were pretty much under control. She didn't have to go to church with us because she's Catholic, which I later understood was a major upset in the family since my grandparents were Nixon lovers who had no use for anyone the same religion as JFK.

Not that Mom was a good Catholic—she never went to Mass or anything, which was fine with me because frankly the last thing I needed was another church to be dragged to. And of course, my father conveniently worked on Sunday mornings, which not only excused him from church, but got him away from all the kids and the Jesus-screaming wife.

Nana and Papa were awesome grandparents, the kind who'd cut the crust off our bread and let us stay up as late as we wanted when we slept at their house. They were in with the Methodist "in crowd." Nana was active in the women's craft group that made stuff out of egg cartons and plastic Clorox bottles to sell at the monthly rummage sale. Papa was an usher and they let him collect money when it was that time in the service.

I felt a little guilty about hating church, since they were so into it, but even as a ten-year-old, I felt terribly phony sitting there and found the worshipping concept a bit eerie. All the hymns and the stained glass images of Jesus and his friends kind of freaked me out. To this day, I'm uncomfortable with religious music and pictures of religious figures, although I'm sure they'd be very nice if you knew them.

How I fought with my mother every Sunday morning! In retrospect, I realize she was just trying to satisfy the in-laws, since she was only marginally on their good side anyway for being Catholic and all. But church was not for me. Sometimes to fight my boredom, I'd fill in my name and address on the little cards on the back of the pew, not realizing I was requesting home visits from the minister. After my mother figured out why he kept showing up at the house unexpectedly—and calling her "Linda"—I didn't have to go to church anymore.

And now here I am, sitting in church of my own free will. This place isn't too scary. This strip mall church has chairs instead of pews, and instead of stained glass windows, there are framed pictures on the wall, which my eyes avoid. I hope there's no music.

The service begins and a distinguished looking gray-haired man starts speaking. He's an eloquent communicator and hardly ever mentions Jesus. I'm pleased to be here even though the air is stale.

The topic of today's sermon is "How to Be a Compatible Person." Although I fancy myself as already quite compatible—*I'm* not the one with the problems—I'm open to suggestions. Pastor Man directs us to a list of affirmations in our program, which he encourages us to recite during our personal meditation time at home.

"I radiate peace, love, and healing to others." Closing my eyes I imagine Bastard Husband in New Zealand, happy to be in his homeland. I cannot bring myself to radiate peace and love. No, he's the one who should be sitting here learning how to be a more com-

patible person.

"I am able to sense another person's needs." That's easy—obviously he needs help. But my sense of superiority ends with the next thought that jumps into my brain from nowhere: he needs love. The truth I feel in that sobers me. I offer a defensive response to my own revelation: No one loves him like I do, and that hasn't been enough.

"I am compassionate when someone is truly suffering." I think of the mornings I'd find him asleep at the kitchen table, slumped over the incriminations of the night before: a 12-pack of empties he'd knocked over, perhaps a half-eaten chicken carcass, a crushed pack of cigarettes beside a full ashtray, some heavy metal CDs, and scribbles of philosophical insights he could conjure up only while under the charm of alcohol. I'd turn off the light above the sink and steer him to the bedroom, where he'd snore for another hour or two before emerging with the look that acknowledged another broken promise. No one would choose a life of perpetual guilt, the result of one's own collapsed willpower. I know he suffers.

I put on my sunglasses to hide my eyes. I wish I had a Kleenex.

The ushers pass the collection plates, and I'm happy to give. Then things take a dreadful turn as we are asked to hold the hands of the persons on either side of us. I reluctantly link with two complete strangers, imagining the transfer of germs. And, *shit*, they want us to sing.

"Let there be peace on earth and let it begin with me," everyone starts in. Everyone but me. Note to self: if I ever come back, sneak out before the singing starts. I'm not one for audience participation. Why can't I just sit here?

After the service some of us check out the New Age bookstore set up in a room off the sanctuary. I scan the titles, many of which I already own—*Embracing the Beloved, Personal Power Through Awareness, Divine Guidance*—and wish they carried the book I'd really like to read: *Smack Some Sense into that Bastard Husband.*

A pleasant man strikes up a conversation. His name is Danny, he's from Springfield, Missouri, and is considering moving to Vegas. He's a healer, he tells me.

"I'm going to stay for the singles group at one o'clock," he says. "How about you? Are you single?"

Am I single? I respond with a vacuous look. On paper, I am. But no, I'm still attached. I love him, I want him to stop drinking, and I want him to come back to me. Although maybe I'd have better luck meeting someone in church instead of a bar.

"No, I'm married," I tell him, presenting my wedding ring as proof. "My husband's visiting his family in New Zealand."

Small talk ensues. *Oh, yes, I've been there. It's very nice. He's a professor; he has the summer off. He'll be back in August.* How accomplished and exotic sounding, and no one has to know the unpleasant details.

After all these years, I'm still a phony in church.

§ § §

I decide to call him after dinner—which is a bowl of cereal—and early into the conversation I know I've made a mistake. His polite but distant tone annoys me.

"I have a friend who's looking for a housemate, so I'll be moving out of Mum's," he says, as if he's reporting the weather. I interpret that arrangement to mean he won't be returning to the northern hemisphere. *Did you quit your job in Utah?* I want to ask, but respond with a deep breath and a simple, "Oh."

Goddamn him. I try to keep it under the surface, but as we speak I can hear the bitchiness seep into my voice, and when you hear it yourself, you know the other person does, too. To think that today

45

in church I actually tried to be loving and compassionate. Now I couldn't care less about his stupid healing. Fine, stay out of my life, you fucking drunk.

8.

I'm starting to make a friend—Mona, from my divorce support group. She's the one who spent twenty-seven years with someone who, I've concluded, utterly repulsed her. A few days ago she found some suspicious looking receipts, including a canceled check made out to a middle school in California, and now she's wondering whether there's been more going on with her future ex than a mid-life crisis.

I like Mona. She reminds me of my strong-willed Jewish girl-friends from high school. I can't imagine her taking any crap, but she must have. The separation seems like it's been a long time coming.

"Did you know your husband was an alcoholic before you married him?" she asked in the parking lot after our meeting last Tuesday night.

"Yeah, I did."

Her face twisted in confusion. "And you married him anyway?"

"Yup." I looked her in the eye. "Did you know your husband was an asshole before you married him?"

She nodded slowly. "Yup."

§ § §

My heart raced as I waited for the Laramie police to arrive. *Did I do the right thing?* I wondered. *Maybe he's not as bad as I thought.*

I met the two female officers at the front door and closed it behind me. "I think everything's under control now," I said, shivering in the overnight chill. "I probably don't need you after all."

"Where is he now, ma'am?" the taller woman asked. I'd put her at about five-foot three. Talk about a small police department. Good thing I didn't fear for my life.

"In the basement," I replied. "There's a little room with a couch. He's settling down now. I probably didn't need to call. I'm sorry to bother you."

"We'd like to speak to him, ma'am," the other one said.

I could tell they had no intention of leaving, so I let them into the house and led them through the kitchen to the stairs.

"Why don't you stay here," one of them advised in a question that wasn't a question. The two of them trudged down the steps and after a moment, the blasting Iron Maiden CD shut off mid-scream.

I remained in the kitchen, mentally trying to justify the call. I had kind of expected a blowout that night, since the day marked the last day of classes. He was particularly vulnerable when something came to an end, whether it was the semester, a paper he'd written for an academic journal, or sometimes simply the end of the week. All ends seemed to lead to the deep end.

I knew the pattern well. The beers in the first stage of intoxication inspired brilliant philosophical revelations, invariably related to harness racing or the stock market. During Stage Two, he loved me deeply, and would even wake me from a sound sleep to profess his adoration. "I'm the luckiest guy, babe," he'd say. "You're the woman for me. You understand me."

And then there was Stage Three.

Somehow between the eighth and tenth beers the most perfect woman on earth inexplicably morphed into a white trash whore who should be eternally grateful to be married to an amazing guy like him. He would sometimes accompany the tirade with a peculiar, and extremely annoying, practice of pouring water on me in bed. Water doesn't leave a mark, but believe me, it can scar.

Often when events unfolded like that, I'd leave before the situation got too ugly. But on that night I wanted to sleep in my own bed. I'd already taken my contacts out, and wasn't up to facing a puzzled front desk clerk remarking on the fact that I was checking into a motel three blocks from my house.

I should have left anyway; I should have recognized the new level of aggression, the way he followed me around, pressing his weight into me and shouting, "You can't control me!" "You fucking bitch!" and other selections from his greatest inebriated hits. He'd never been physically violent, but the behavior that night scared me. I didn't want to risk what could happen if his mood escalated. Mostly I worried he might accidentally shove me into something or send me flying down the very cellar stairs I'd fantasized about finding his drunken ass at the base of. I thought I was right to call the police. Maybe not.

I listened hard at the top of the stairs, but heard only muffled conversation. *What the hell could they be talking about? He's probably giving them stock tips.*

The women finally made their way back upstairs. I half expected them to tell me he's the greatest guy and I should be thankful to be his wife.

"He's going to stay down there tonight," the smaller one reported. "I think he'll be asleep soon. I doubt you have anything to worry about." She handed me a card with her name and badge number. "I've circled a referral on the back for Project SAFE. They can help you if you need a place to stay. I think you'll be okay for tonight, but you'll have the number in case you need it in the future."

A police officer just gave me a referral to a women's shelter.

"You know, I have a master's degree…" I wanted to say. Instead, I took the card and muttered, "Thank you."

§ § §

The next day I left the house before he woke up, figuring I'd give him some time alone so he could formulate his apology. Following my own morning-after pattern, I drove downtown and walked around to kill some time.

When we first moved to Laramie, I found a quiet contentment in wandering the streets alone on mornings like that, despite the events of the night before. But lately I'd grown weary of the routine, and instead of admiring the restored Wild-West buildings, I dreamed of getting out of Dodge.

Coincidentally Laramie, Wyoming, is in Albany County. As I passed the Albany County Library, I longed to be back in Albany, New York, among the people who loved me, instead of in the middle of the prairie with no one but a miserable drunk.

I walked past the Buckhorn Bar on Ivenson Avenue. We'd stopped in there a few weeks before and had marveled not only at the bullet hole in the mirror behind the bar, but the fact that the bartender continued to serve a staggering local who'd achieved a level of intoxication that even Bastard Husband could only aspire to. Generally slow to progress, Laramie had yet to embrace the concept of alcohol awareness. Drive-thru liquor stores graced every corner and they opened before the Rite-Aid, even on Sundays. Good for people who want to get toasted before church—not so boring that way.

I settled in at the Muddy Waters coffeehouse, a familiar refuge filled with kitschy pop culture posters and toys from the 60s, *the* place to be if you wanted to kick ass on a vintage *Addams Family* board game. I took in the assortment of old hippie-types, students, and some regular folks drinking their herbal teas and coffee concoctions, all strangers I'd never get to know. Although the people of Laramie were the nicest I'd ever met, I deliberately made no attempt to make friends. As a "trailing spouse" to a visiting professor filling a one-year vacancy, I arrived with the understanding that I'd be there for just a short time. Why start friendships only to move on?

I must say, I left Albany without hesitation. My kids were in their twenties and by that point, the foundation had been laid—if they were going to be serial killers, there wasn't a thing I could do about it. And although I hated to leave my precious little grandson, I felt in my heart it was my time, my time for an adventure. I'd lived in the same general neighborhood for over forty-three years!

Besides, I'd been drawn to the West my whole life; as a kid my imaginary friends were cowboys and sheriffs. I often told people, proudly and with absolute certainty, that in a former life I was a saloon girl. It made total sense, given my childhood obsession with *Bonanza* and my comfort level as an adult in the tavern environment. Not to mention my passion for lipstick. Then a couple of years ago someone took me aside and told me, to my surprise, that those women were prostitutes. Although I remain quite certain of that past life, I now keep the admission to myself.

Even though we'd been married for several months by the time we got to Laramie, the move marked the first we actually lived together. Before that, I worked on the road during the week, and we split our weekends between his apartment in Buffalo and my house in Albany. Our possessions finally merged in the U-Haul, which he loaded, drove cross-country, and unloaded in flip flops—jandels, as they call them in New Zealand. We had great fun setting up our rented bungalow, and I carefully protected my sensitive Jackson Browne and Leonard Cohen CDs from his raucous Ozzy Osbourne and Venom. I never thought I'd have to protect myself.

After a couple of hours of people-watching and three decaf mocha lattes, I decided to head home, expecting to be met with the typical avoiding glances. Usually the intensity of the night before dictated the length of time until we spoke, and considering I had called the cops on him, I figured it would be quite a while before we exchanged words.

I entered an empty house. He'd cleaned up the bottles and cigarette butts, which was usually my chore. A note on the dining room table read, "Went to school to grade papers. Check your email."

I got online.

> *"Honey,*
> *I feel embarrassed and sad about what happened. My lack of self-esteem is a problem. I never thought I would be with someone like you. Part of me doesn't believe I deserve you and wants to self-destruct by drinking. Part of me hates you for growing me into a better person. The drinking creeps up in such an innocent way. I don't connect to where it's going to lead. That's why I'm going to stop completely. I'll make it my priority in life."*

Too physically and emotionally exhausted to deal with his message or anything else, I went to the bedroom and lay down next to a pile of folded laundry. Well, his version of folding. I must have slept, though it seemed no time had passed. I didn't hear him come in, but I felt the bed sag when he sat next to me.

"I'm sorry about last night, eh," he said softly.

I opened my eyes and looked up at him, unable to muster an expression.

"Why did you call the police on me?" he asked, not looking at me, but at the clothes.

"You scared me." I didn't offer details. Silence. For a while.

"I, uh . . ." He sighed as he struggled to put words together, his left eyebrow arching and quivering. *What now?* I wondered.

Taking a deep breath, he looked away and let it rip. "I shrunk your clothes, eh."

Fully awake now, I gave him a look that said, *What the hell are you talking about?*

"The wash that was in the machine...I put it in the dryer." His expression was that of a little boy who'd smacked a baseball through a neighbor's window. "Look," he said, presenting Exhibit A, a black stretchy top that looked perfectly normal to me. "Everything shrunk. I'm sorry, babe. I guess I shouldn't have dried them."

"You didn't shrink anything," I said. "My clothes can be dried; they're just small compared to yours." *Duh.* As I watched the blood return to his face, I realized I'd never actually seen the diploma for his Ph.D.

We hugged for a long time, an embrace that both celebrated his relief and acknowledged the unspoken ruins of the previous night. He stunk from the inside out, the toxins still escaping from his pores. I hoped none of his colleagues at school had gotten a whiff of him.

"I took some salmon out of the freezer," he said, "I'll make some broccoli, too. I want to get healthy."

"I know you do."

"You feel like doing some yoga first?" he asked. After we disentangled ourselves, I looked him over. How could he possibly be up for yoga? Then as if he read my mind, he added, "Something easy, eh."

We did our yoga together. I watched him huff and puff as the sweat dripped onto his mat. God help him, I thought. He's trying.

9.

My refrigerator makes me sad. I counted them today—thirty-three magnets, souvenirs of our trips together, representations of the good life.

Some came from cities: Seattle, Montreal, New Orleans, Auckland. Some from more obscure destinations: Jerome, Arizona; Taos, New Mexico; Deadwood, South Dakota. Then there's our national park collection: Arches, Joshua Tree, Rocky Mountain, and our old neighborhood playgrounds, Bryce and Zion.

Whenever I get a bowl of ice cream, which is now four times a day—two during my soap and two whenever the hell I want—I'm reminded of the fun we had traveling together. Are those days truly over?

§ § §

Alcoholics, I've learned, drown themselves in a spiral of guilt, shame, self-hatred and denial. I respected his courage in Laramie to claim his offenses and look them straight in the eye. He didn't mean to act like such a bastard, and I believed him when he said he wanted to stop drinking more than anything.

During his sober periods, life was never better. His academic schedule allowed for lots of time off, time his colleagues might have spent doing research, but time we used to explore the West. We had no house to maintain, no chores to tend to, nothing to fix or paint. Instead we'd go for a hike or drive down to Boulder, Colorado, for the weekend to take in a yoga class. We traveled every chance we could.

I loved our road trips. We racked up thousands of miles through the sparse landscape of Wyoming, the mountains of Colorado, the deserts of California and Arizona. We hit every western state but Oregon, talking for hours on end, never once listening to music. He had an abundance of philosophies to impart, and I loved listening to him. I appreciated his loquaciousness, especially since my first husband, God bless him, was practically mute.

We had all the time and money to do anything we wanted—what a change from my first marriage. Whereas in the early days Chris and I searched the couch cushions or raided the kids' piggy banks for money for the next meal, B.H. and I shopped in the giant grocery warehouses, returning home with enough food for a month, toilet paper to last the whole semester, and a five-year supply of Spray-N-Wash.

Best of all, I didn't have to work—where could I work in Laramie anyway? My job was to take care of him, and that was the only job I ever had that I actually enjoyed. I remember pulling clothes out of the washer one morning after he left for school and noticing I'd successfully rubbed a stain from one of his newer shirts. (Obviously I had the resources.) The point is, I knew he'd be pleased. That simple accomplishment brought me tons more satisfaction than any of the crap on my resume.

Taking advantage of my time away from the corporate world, I decided to pursue the credentials I needed to become a certified yoga teacher, something I'd wanted to do for a while. After researching several programs I settled on a yoga school on a Hindu ashram outside of Austin, Texas.

I should have looked up "ashram" in the dictionary before I spent the longest ten days of my life living on one. We had no TV, no newspaper, no contact with the outside world. My multitude of neuroses surfaced front and center. The first night, I asked an instructor for paper off a flipchart so I could cover the pictures that hung in my room of Lord Krishna and Lord Vishnu (and all four of his arms). I then had to explain my phobia of religious images—even the American ones, I assured her, so she wouldn't think I was the prejudiced type. I kind of felt like a baby, but how was I supposed to sleep with those two watching me?

And the food. I'm a picky eater—I was eighteen before I tried cream cheese and thirty-six before I ate a chick pea. One. I wouldn't live long enough to try the curried God-knows-what they were dishing out in the dining hall. I begged one of my fellow trainees who had a car on site to sneak me off to a grocery store, where I loaded up on treasures such as macadamia nuts, chips and salsa, and mint Milano cookies. So instead of wanting to cry at mealtimes, I'd calmly push a glob of rice crap around my plate, then run upstairs to my closet and feast on my contraband like a crazed bulimic.

After I let a couple of my more sympathetic comrades in on my secret, I'd find them at my door when their cravings kicked in. Our little snack parties on the floor under the covered pictures of the Hindu gods reminded me of smoking pot with friends in my dorm room in Plattsburgh while grooving to *Dark Side of the Moon*. Except we were supposed to be mature students of a highly spiritual practice.

When I got back to Laramie, I started a yoga program at a gym in town, and also set up classes for young people with Down syndrome. I loved teaching them, even the woman who copped a feel every time she hugged me. There was a boyfriend and girlfriend in the class, and I remember thinking it must be nice to be in a relationship where your biggest complaint is that he doesn't share his Skittles. How I hated to say good-bye to those gentle souls when it came time to move on. I still think of them often.

Before his gig in Laramie ended, Bastard Husband secured a tenure-track position at a university in southwest Utah. Even though the school's reputation was distinctively less than competitive, we felt good about the move; the hiking would be incredible and after a year in Wyoming, neither of us cared to return to the frenzied lifestyle of the East.

In the weeks before we packed up, he was in the "I've quit drinking, this time for good" mode, which to his credit, had lasted longer than previous attempts. As we pulled into our new town, my heart filled with hope. Surely living in the Mormon culture would support his dedication to sobriety. Whereas alcohol flowed freely in Wyoming, a whole different Jesus ran the show in Utah, and from what I understood, he didn't take kindly to boozing.

Just after we unloaded the last box off the U-Haul, our doorbell rang. We looked at each other with dread.

"Oh, Christ," I said, rolling my eyes. "Those Mormons don't waste any time, do they?"

Navigating around the mess of boxes, I mentally rehearsed my "Don't Even Try to Convert Us" speech. I opened the door to find a smiling couple about my age.

"Hi, I'm Mary," said the woman. "This is my husband, Sam. We live next door. We wanted to bring over a little housewarming present. I know you're busy unpacking, so we won't stay."

I offered my hand to Mary. "Hi, I'm Linda." They looked pretty cool, but I maintained my guard in case the topic suddenly turned to religion.

In a man-to-man gesture, Sam offered the gift to my husband. "I hope you drink beer," he said.

The guy marking his fifth straight week of sobriety opened the bag and pulled out a twelve-pack. "Oh yeah, thanks," he said. "That's really nice."

"It's Polygamy Porter," Sam explained, "a Utah microbrew. Don't get too excited, it's only three percent. They have some crazy rules here about alcohol content."

We exchanged pleasantries for a few minutes. I smiled appropriately as I processed the encounter, vacillating between relief that they weren't missionaries and disbelief that we received the gift of alcohol within two hours of arriving in the empire of the Latter Day Saints.

"Don't you think it's kind of weird that they came over with beer?" I asked after our neighbors left. "We could have been Mormons. How did they know?"

B.H. put his arm around me and said, "Remember when you scraped your leg getting the TV stand off the truck?"

"Yeah."

He stood close and whispered, "Mormons don't yell, 'Fuck!'"

We smiled into each other's eyes. Another new adventure.

He kissed me on the cheek. "You can have that beer, eh. I'm not drinking anymore, babe."

Two days later, a retired man from across the street who must have also caught wind of my vulgarity brought over a six-pack of Killians. And the following Friday night, the sober streak came to an end.

Once again I realized no matter how well he seemed to be doing, the other shoe would inevitably drop. I could never trust my happiness. And whatever hope I had would inevitably be deflated. Hope can be a virtue or a curse. I heard that once on *Guiding Light*.

10.

Our life in Cedar City mirrored the landscape. In contrast to the barren countryside around Laramie, which at times took on the color of dust, Utah was vivid, like someone adjusted the tint on the TV. Everything, not just the scenery, became more intense for us—the highs higher, the lows lower.

On the plus side, I could sit on my couch and look out at beautiful red rocks. The nearby hiking was nothing short of spectacular, and again, there were no corporate opportunities in such a small town, so I set up some yoga classes.

Best of all, I found it easy to make friends. The non-Mormons in town seemed to have their radar on for cool people to hang out with and in no time, I got in with some fun, high-spirited women who shared my interest in metaphysics.

I met Becky first, at a biofeedback lecture given by Dr. Turner, the finger-pulling psychic healer I eventually worked for. The topic of his talk was secondary to my need to get out of the house that night. Becky taught women's studies at the university and she's the one who introduced me to the rest of the girls.

I immediately loved them all, and got the biggest kick out of Michael—a female Michael, Michael Mahoney—though this Michael Mahoney was nothing like the image one might conjure of a strapping red-faced jokester at the end of the bar. And in contrast to sweet Becky, who no doubt wore the same long hair and flowing skirts thirty years ago in high school, Michael, a dead-ringer for Martha Stewart, dressed in nothing but classic designers and was the only woman in Cedar City who bothered with panty hose.

A native of Los Angeles, Michael had moved to Utah several years before, also as a trailing spouse, as we're called. She hated Utah, and to make matters worse, her third husband had recently left her for another woman, which accounted for her perpetually distracted look. Michael was sarcastic and cynical, and when she cooly dragged on a cigarette, I half expected the exhaled smoke to form the words "Fuck off" in the air above her. Although I usually find negative people repelling, her pissiness struck me as quite endearing.

A few of us would meet as a group every other Sunday night, ostensibly to explore a topic related to spiritual growth. Invariably, however, the conversation digressed into a not-so-open minded discussion on living in a community comprised of seventy percent Mormons.

As the new kid, I'd start things rolling, if for no other reason than to release the shellshock. "It's weird being in the minority," I said at one of our gatherings. "Now I know why the black kids sat together in the high school cafeteria."

"A black person…Yes, I see them on TV." Michael's wonderful sarcasm.

I had to brag. "I saw one in the parking lot at Albertson's the other day."

"You did not!"

"I did, too!" I said, in mock self-defense. "Seriously, I feel like I'm on a social scavenger hunt here." I proudly rattled off some of my finds to date, counting them on my fingers. "So far I've met a nice lesbian couple, a woman who married and divorced the same man three times, and a Jew." I paused for dramatic effect as the girls exchanged glances. "Not a New York Jew—I wish!—but a Jew in Utah nonetheless. That should count for something. Speaking of . . . What I would give for a decent bagel shop."

"What I would give for a decent coffee shop," my new friend Lynn pined.

"I'd even take a Starbucks and all its perverse corporate glory!" Coming from Becky, our activist hippie chick, that was quite a statement.

"Get used to it. Coffee is evil here," said Michael.

"Not to mention alcohol," Becky added.

"What? You don't like drinking the piss-water they try to pass off as beer?" Michael asked, gazing off at nothing. Lynn nodded. As an alcohol counselor, she understood the difference between real beer and piss water.

"No, and I don't like drinking at Applebees, either."

"I wish we had a good bar where you could go for a night out on the town—have a few drinks, listen to a band..." I said. But then I thought for a moment and added, "It's probably just as well."

The room became quiet. I'd met these women only a short time before, but I'd let them in on what was going on at home. Lynn asked, "How's he doing?"

I shook my head. "He's great today; we had a blast hiking in Zion this afternoon. But that doesn't mean he'll be great when I get home tonight. Just when I think he's doing well, he'll walk in with a six-pack, and have a twelve-pack hidden in the garage. I never know what to expect. It's like he's holding the remote control of our life and I just react to whatever channel he wants to be on."

She offered a knowing nod.

"Lynn, does anyone ever get cured?" I asked. "Do people ever stop drinking and put their life back together?"

"Yes, I've had clients who stop drinking and they become who they really are, who they were meant to be. Miracles can happen. People can change."

People *can* change, I had to believe. And in her line of work, so did Lynn.

I adored those women and appreciated their much-needed support. Bastard Husband's blowouts had become more frequent and angrier, prompting me to seek refuge in a new set of neighborhood motels. He had built up his endurance, too, no longer crashing at three or four a.m., but sometimes lasting until seven, eight, or later. And one time he poured cold coffee on me in bed instead of water. That really pissed me off—I had just changed the sheets.

The ugliness of one particular sleepless night continued well into the next morning, ending with a nasty exchange of our favorite obscenities and my slamming the door as I left the house. Shaking from anger and exhaustion, I drove to the nursing home where I volunteered to teach a nine o'clock yoga class to the residents. Thank God they're in wheelchairs, I thought. I had created a seated yoga program for them, and if I were to teach a power yoga class at that point, I'd have put myself into cardiac arrest.

I pulled up to the single-story building on the edge of town and checked myself out in the rear view mirror before entering. I looked like hell, but who doesn't look like hell in a rear view mirror?

The aides had assembled everyone in the recreation area, a gaily decorated room with several couches, a piano, and a large screen TV. We had a good crowd that morning, maybe fifteen residents, all dressed for the day and eyeing me with anticipation. "They love doing their yoga," the volunteer coordinator once told me.

"Good morning, everyone!" I sang as I walked in. I stopped to hug a couple of them as I made my way to the chair up front. "I'm so happy to see you all today!" I meant that.

I put on a Native American CD of calming flute music, and led them in a deep breathing exercise, mainly to regulate my own still furiously pounding heart. I watched them close their eyes and breathe with intention, as I had instructed. I studied their beautiful faces, lined with the expressions of their lives, and felt happy that they would never know my last words before coming to class had been, "I'll cut your fucking dick off!"

Despite all the bullshit, I never gave up on him. When things were good, I honestly believed there was no better person on earth for me, no one I was more meant to be with.

But I could feel him slipping away. The morning-after expressions of tender apology and profound self-insight gradually faded. The post-blowout recovery time grew longer and longer, often stretching to two or three days before we spoke again. Sometimes he'd drive down to Mesquite, a town on the Utah-Nevada border, or he'd spend the weekend in Las Vegas. Either place allowed him to mix the gambling dynamic with the drinking.

Sometimes I swore he picked fights when he wasn't drinking just so he could take off like that. A casual remark out of my mouth would erupt into a major battle, with him reciting a list of every sin I had ever committed, starting with my calling the police on him that night in Laramie.

If I asked him about something twice, I was a nagging bitch. That pissed me off to no end. I know men don't like to be nagged, but for God's sake, there's a difference between nagging and "reminding." Nagging, I believe, is self-inflicted and totally preventable—if he'd done what I asked the first time, there'd be no reason to nag. It's as simple as that.

The point was, shit could hit the fan at any moment, and for any reason. I started to doubt my own perceptions: Maybe I *was* a bitch. Maybe *I* was the one with the problem.

11.

Another email yesterday—again, all business. Like I give a crap about his precious *Economist*. He never offers a hint of emotion; all his correspondence is devoid of human expression.

He said that next week he's interviewing at the university in Christchurch on New Zealand's south island. Last week he presented a paper at a school in Hamilton, which supposedly went very well. Those aren't exactly indications that he intends to come back. I'd love to know whether he quit his job in Utah yet, but I won't ask. The new semester starts in three weeks.

I miss him, and as time passes I realize I'm starting to forget the dysfunctional parts of our relationship. I miss the good husband— the adorable, fun-loving absent-minded professor. I forget about the bastard husband—the insecure, miserable, controlling asshole I put up with in the months before he left.

My mother just called. I can tell she knows something's up. I've let some things slip, no doubt. Like my concern about getting a job—why would I be so worried if I had his income to rely on? I also notice I talk in terms of "I" instead "we" lately. This sucks.

I wonder if he's still wearing his wedding ring.

Lately I'm getting more and more into meditation. God knows I have the time and frankly I don't feel like doing anything but sit around anyway, so I might as well be productive. I'm noticing results, particularly an increase in intuition. I actually do feel guided. Not that I hear voices or anything, but sometimes I get a burst of thought that doesn't quite come from my own brain. It's hard to clear your mind of its endless self-talk, particularly when you have so much crap going on in your life, but as I understand it, that's the only way guidance can come through. Makes sense—you can't listen if you're chattering away.

Meditation is pretty cool. I can see how it helps to instill a sense of peace. Sometimes I think of his face and send him love. I know in my heart that everything is unfolding exactly as it should. All is well.

§ § §

My printer is all fucked up! I have to print out my resume for an interview this afternoon. To sell timeshares—yeah, I need a master's degree for that. I don't know what's wrong; I don't know a goddamn thing about printers, but I do know this one is a piece of shit so I charged a new one on my Visa this morning. Then I had to go back to the store because I needed some goddamn piece of something that plugs into the back of the computer, an adapter maybe?

I glare at the printer and all the connecting crap I've dumped out of the box. This is *his* job.

Fuck! I hate him! It's all his fault I have to deal with these goddamn wires. That mother fucking bastard! How could he just walk out of my life like I'm some goddamn bit of… whatever he doesn't need anymore? What did he think? *Oh, I'm going to New Zealand. I might come back, I might not. We'd better get divorced, though, just in case. Til death do us part? Um, sorry, I didn't mean that.*

Fucker! I have used every spiritual coping mechanism in my repertoire and frankly I'm sick of trying to approach this from a "higher place." Yes, intellectually I understand God is not looking at him saying, "You're absolutely right, Linda. He *is* a mother-fucking bastard. I screwed up on that one," but I'm tired of trying to be forgiving and all that bullshit. I don't want to start over, I don't want to take some crappy job selling timeshares and I don't want to fuck around with this computer—I don't know where anything gets plugged in.

I give his picture the finger, the picture of the two of us on top of Medicine Bow. I wonder if I've gained any weight since that was taken. I don't think so.

I am not mechanically inclined. I don't know how to fix anything—I'm lucky I can get self-service gas. I fancy myself as having all the patience in the world for people, but I could take a fucking hammer to a machine that doesn't do what I want it to.

Some of the women in my divorce support group mention how they call their exes to come to the house when an appliance breaks down. I don't blame them—I used to do it all the time after Chris and I split up. Sometimes I really needed something to be looked at, but I wasn't above dramatizing the situation a bit, creating an emergency that needed his immediate attention to conveniently take him away from his new girlfriend.

Back to the task at hand. Okay, it might not be too bad—only four pages of instructions. My cable TV service came with a 128-page booklet—textbook, I should say—and I did manage to figure out how to automatically record *Guiding Light* everyday without having to call the cable company for help. Maybe I can do this.

I carefully unplug the old printer. Following the step-by-step instructions, and with surprisingly minimal confusion, I manage to find the correct plugs for the new printer. I insert the accompanying CD and click away as prompted, ever so cautiously, as if one wrong move will accidentally start a nuclear war from my apartment.

Click …click…good, just keep letting me click. Now what? *Cartridges?* Why does this have to be so complicated?

Finally it wants me to run a test page, I guess to make sure I did everything right. Oh, please God, let this fucking thing print out okay. No, wait…What should I say? *I am sending positive vibrations to my printer.* I click one last time, and…success! I watch the new printer perform obediently and fold my arms with such pride and self-importance you'd think I discovered a cure for cellulite. Who can I call? I feel like bragging.

"You've got mail!" my computer announces, interrupting my gloating.

It's from Bastard Husband. Great. He's probably still worrying about his stupid subscription. I open his message.

"Linda, I've been thinking about you a great deal. If I were to come back, would you still have me?"

My mind tries to process the unexpected query. After a while I lean into his words on the screen and shout, "I don't need you! I did it myself!"

I sit back, an idiotic smile broadcasting my smug face to no one. Soooo, he wants to come back.

§ § §

The stylish man with the slicked hair on the other side of the desk is describing the in's and out's of "vacation ownership." At least I think he is; I don't know for sure. I can't understand a word he says, but I suppose a job interview is not the place to tell someone to take the fucking marbles out of his mouth.

He holds a pen in front of me. "Sell me this pen!" he commands, grinning like an imbecile.

Kiss my ass. I don't want to play his stupid game. In fact, I don't want to play the whole "I Need to Find a Job" game at all. I've been here over two months and have not generated a single interview worth the effort of putting on a suit and pantyhose. I've filled out a slew of online applications, most of them assaulting me with an error message when I hit the "Submit" button, and the ones that did go through have yet to result in any kind of acknowledgment. Last week I wasted over an hour at an employment agency transferring the exact crap from my resume into little boxes on a four-page application and then fumed in the waiting area until finally I was granted a thirty-second encounter with an overly-bleached blonde in a too-short skirt who knew nothing about the training position posted on their website and who advised me to consider deleting my master's degree from my resume since employers in Las Vegas are "not really looking for people with that much education."

I'm not surprised. Where do educated people work here? You don't need a degree to valet cars, dispense cocktails, or deal blackjack. And contrary to Albany, where there are four universities, a medical school, a law school, and a pharmacy college within 10 miles of downtown, this place has only UNLV, the University of Nevada Las Vegas, which is probably comparable to Plattsburgh State, where I attended undergrad. However, there does appear to be a multitude of post-secondary trade schools, the kind you see advertised during *The Simpsons*.

I certainly don't need a degree to sell timeshares. I want to walk out, but I inhale deeply and take the pen from Mr. Bryll-Cream. Sell you this pen? Okay...A load of bullshit tumbles from my mouth. He seems pleased, but I'd feel less disgraced if I'd just blown him under the table.

On the way home, I try to liberate myself from the nasty aftertaste by thinking positive thoughts. *Maybe I won't have to go through this anymore. Maybe things will be different when he gets back. I won't have to take a shit job. I can teach yoga and we'll take our trips on his semester breaks and we'll be in love again.*

My cell phone rings the minute I walk into the apartment. They'd like to offer me a position as a vacation sales counselor.

"Thank you," I say, "but I don't think I'm a good match for the position. Thank you for your time."

I return to the computer and pull up his email message from earlier in the day: "If I were to come back, would you still have me?" I consider his words for one final moment before typing in, "Yes."

SEND.

PART II

1.

"Where do you go when you go out? What do you do? Tell me! I have to know these things." Mona wildly fans away a hot flash while devouring her Caesar salad. Lately we've been meeting for dinner on Tuesday nights before our group. Her stash of two-for-one coupons comes in handy, since each of our financial situations is tenuous these days.

"It's no big deal," I say. "I find out what's going on in the weekly arts magazine, figure out how to get there, then hop in the car and go." The entertainment paper and a map are essential tools for building a life in a new city.

"You mean you go to bars? Alone?"

"Yeah." I detect faint disapproval in her tone, but reply without the matching hint of defensiveness. "Irish bars are the best. People are friendly. They like to talk and they're not out to pick you up." And, I want to add, what are the chances of meeting another alcoholic in a place like that?

She frowns. I didn't expect her to share my enthusiasm for all things Celtic, but I enjoy imagining a nice Jewish woman at the height of menopause tying one on to "Whiskey in the Jar." I should tell her about that little bit of salad dressing on her face, but I don't know her well enough.

"I found an interesting place just west of the Strip," I continue. "Boomers—it's a bar that has open mic comedy in their back room on Sunday nights."

"Is that something you'd like to do?"

"Hell, no!" I shoot back, still scarred from Johnny Carson rejecting my Captain Hook and Moby Dick jokes. If Johnny wasn't impressed, I must have no comedic talent.

I've been going to Boomers every Sunday night for the past several weeks. It's interesting—I've never lived anywhere that had open mic comedy. The place is kind of a hole, but that's okay. They have an emcee and a DJ who plays music as the comics walk up to the stage. Usually about seven or eight people perform, mostly all young guys in their twenties, a few might be older.

"I was with Alan for twenty-eight years, and my friends have their husbands to go out with," Mona says. "I never go anywhere by myself. I wouldn't know what to do. You have to help me. You're my only single friend."

"No problem. I'll teach you." I don't consider myself single, but *I'm her friend*. I have a friend here now!

"Go like this," I tell her, rubbing the left side of my cheek with my napkin.

§ § §

I like to make the scene; there's no way I can sit around my apartment every night. And because of my years on the road, I'm used to going out alone. But sometimes even I have to push myself to hit the town. If I lack confidence for whatever reason (usually related to my weight or hair), I can easily spend an evening on the couch weeping over my video of Princess Di's funeral. I'm heading out tonight, though. I'm on my way to Boulder Station, a casino on the east side of town that advertises blues bands every Thursday night, national acts with no cover charge. Dan, the guy I met in line at the DMV, told me about this place. I asked Mona if she wanted to join me, but she has to work tomorrow.

I've put together a cute little outfit—a black miniskirt and a funky tank top that looks like something I once borrowed from my college roommate that's back in style now. At least I *think* it's in style. I don't know. I need my daughter—Courtney will always alert me to a fashion faux pas I have no idea I've committed. The last time I visited Albany, she stopped me at the door as I left to meet a couple of girlfriends for drinks.

"Mom!" she cried, her head developing a Parkinsons-like shake. "Those pants!"

"What do you mean?" I asked, totally not getting it. How could these stretch denim hip-hugger bell bottoms be anything but cute? Then a horrific thought shot me into panic. "What? Do these make me look fat?"

"No, but they look like something Marlee would wear." Marlee is my niece. She just finished middle school.

The truth is, I do shop in the Junior section of the department store, where Marlee and her friends get their wardrobes. I still fit in those clothes, and if I like them, I buy them, regardless of what someone forty-five years old "should" be wearing. Besides, most of what I see in the grown-up ladies' section looks kind of farty, and I like to look cute.

Cute is good! When I get old I want to be the cutest lady in the assisted living facility. I'll prance around in my cute little orthopedic shoes and cute little housedress, which I'll hem into a miniskirt, and anyone who doesn't like my ninety-six-year-old kneecaps can kiss my ass.

I wore those denim hip-hugger bellbottoms out that night. My girlfriends thought they were cute.

§ § §

Boulder Station is easy to find—right off the highway. Whenever I go to a casino, I try to park under the huge, billion-watt sign tempting drivers with their $6.95 prime rib special. That way I have a better chance of finding my car later on. I hate it when I forget where I've parked. Though I'm good at feigning self-assurance while I walk aimlessly down the aisle for twenty minutes, I can't seem to hide that relieved expression of recognition when I finally spot my vehicle.

The ceiling inside the casino is painted to resemble a blue sky that suggests neither day nor night. Obviously phony, yet intriguing—a description that applies to almost everything Vegas. Like the boobs on the woman who just passed me.

Implants. I have to wonder, why? With the superior bra technology these days, anyone can have a nice rack. Who needs to lug giant breasts around 24/7 when all it takes is a little trip to Victoria's Secret? To me, breasts are an accessory; I put them on when I'm going out, along with my earrings and other jewelry, and at the end of the night, they're back in the drawer and I'm sleeping on my stomach. You can't do that with silicone.

The showroom is called the Railhead. It's a good size—larger than intimate, but by no means cavernous—with a dance floor in front of an elevated stage and two levels of seating. Nice. Too bad there's nothing like this in Albany; I'd love to see my son and his band perform in this type of venue. Christopher started entertaining in coffeehouses while still in high school, and now he plays in clubs with a band behind him, performing his originals and covers of artists like John Prine and Leonard Cohen—music more in line with the taste of my generation than his. I'd be no more proud if he were in med school.

I settle in at the bar off to the left side of the room. I have to remember to tell Mona to always sit at the bar; at least you'll have the bartender to talk to if no one interesting comes along. Tip him well and he'll protect you from the drunks.

As the bartender hands me my beer, shades of purple and red light up the stage and the band members take their places. Perfect timing. I scan the crowd and figure these people must be locals. Not dressed to impress, they look like they're wearing whatever they happened to have on all day. Visitors here have their special "Vegas clothes," exposing body parts that aren't allowed to be seen back in Cincinnati.

A light-skinned black man who appears to be in his sixties heads my way. He is well-dressed in a button-up shirt and slacks, classier than the rest of us. Gold chains adorn his neck. As he gets closer, I conclude not a single drop is left in his bottle of cologne.

He looks me over and offers the results of his assessment.

"You're very pretty," he says.

"It's dark in here," I tease. "You don't want to see me in bright sunshine." A bit of an exaggeration, but you have to admit a dimly lit bar is the best-case scenario as far as lighting goes.

"Now tell me," he says, "Why is such a nice young lady sitting all by herself?"

Not the first time I've heard that either. He seems kind rather than lecherous, so I deem him worthy of an honest response.

"I just moved here and don't know anyone yet, and I'm not the type to stay home when I could be out having fun." I smile and nod as if to indicate that is my final answer.

"And you have no gentleman friend?"

"My husband is away visiting his family for the summer." Half-truth, since I don't actually have a husband.

"My name is Frank," he says, offering his hand.

"Linda." We shake and I'm proud of myself for giving out my real name. Sometimes when I'm not a soap opera star, I'm Peggy... as in Peggy Fleming, the 1968 Olympic gold medalist. Christ, how long ago was that?

"Would you like to dance?" he asks, again offering his hand, palm up this time. Frank is such the gentleman.

"No, I don't dance." Now I'm lying. I love to dance. In fact, back home I'm famous for entertaining party-goers by doing a split at the end of a particularly inspiring Talking Heads song. But I don't feel like dancing tonight. I can't bear the thought of touching anyone, or worse, having someone touch me. The only hands I want on my body are on the other side of the world.

Frank is a little more persistent than I wish he'd be, but finally he is convinced of my preference for inertia and moves on to two women sitting at a nearby high-top table. Their posture indicates they are eager to be approached, and as Frank escorts one of them to the dance floor, I wonder if I, too, have that "open for business" look. I don't think so. I hope not.

I miss having girlfriends around. Right now I particularly miss Julie, one of my best friends from Albany. We've spent endless hours together on adjacent barstools praising Oprah, fantasizing about the cosmetic work we'll have done someday...entranced in girl talk that would make men roll their eyes and thank the Lord for their penises. God, I wish I had a girlfriend here.

"Would you like to dance?"

The invitation takes me by surprise. With my focus directed to the stage, I didn't realize someone was on my other side. I turn to see a beautiful blonde. Stunning, in her early thirties, maybe. She's wearing a plaid miniskirt and a black halter that shows off her toned body. I should pop in my Buns of Steel tape when I get home.

"Would you like to dance?" she asks again.

"Um, no. Thank you, though."

"Later, then" she states, giving me a sly once-over before fusing into the crowd.

The band is rocking. A big fat guy in overalls wails on a harmonica in a way that doesn't disappoint. It must be hard for big fat musicians. I think people expect more from them.

I'll have to tell Mona about the cool, "I'm with the band" persona I put on when I'm out by myself. During one of Christopher's gigs I realized you carry yourself with more confidence if you know someone in the band. That's what you have to do. But of course I don't pretend I'm somebody's mother—duh—I make believe one of the musicians is my boyfriend. Except if none of them is particularly attractive, I pretend we're just friends. It really works. I think the harmonica player is my boyfriend tonight, though I could do without the overalls. I like those beefy boys; I'd take Hoss Cartwright over Little Joe any day.

I sneak a look at the people around me, being careful not to make eye contact. I don't care to dance or converse, I'm happy just to sit here. It's an older crowd, no one looks under thirty. What a great place for people my age, and older, to come out and let loose. Everyone seems happy. Come to think of it, everyone I see in Vegas seems happy. Probably because either they're on vacation or they've moved here from somewhere else; this is where they've chosen to live. Not like in Albany. People seem to live there because, well, they always have.

An older couple is taking over the dance floor. They're from the era when dancers learned actual steps, instead of flailing around independently like most people my age. They look into each other's eyes and seem to anticipate their partner's every move as they twirl each other around. I imagine they've been married thirty-five, forty years. Or maybe they're like Mom and her boyfriend, Jim, who connected later in life. That's probably why they seem so in love. It's nice. He's in black from head to toe and is wearing a cowboy hat; she's a slender woman in dungarees with a flat ass that makes me think being thin in itself isn't going to be enough in my old age. I have a feeling they're Republicans.

"I've never seen you before."

The blonde is back. She doesn't look at me in the same way as my friend Julie, and I know for a fact that Julie never once decided to rest her hand on my forearm. I must have the goofiest look on my face.

"No, this is my first time." Now she's stroking—no, *caressing*—my arm. This certainly is my first time.

"Are you sure you don't want to dance?" She is even more persistent than Frank.

"Thanks," I say. "I'm just going to, um, sit here, and, uh…just watch the band tonight." I'm so cool when *guys* hit on me.

"Let me know if you change your mind," she says with a wink before walking away.

"Thanks! You, too!" I call after her. *You, too?* I hate it when I do that.

I laugh to myself and have a quick word with God, thanking him for his prompt response to my request for a girlfriend and asking why the hell he's not hip to the fact I'm not a lesbian. In the future I'll be a little more specific with my prayers, since evidently his scope of knowledge is not so all-encompassing after all. Though maybe I should reconsider; men don't exactly seem to be working out. Believe me, sometimes I wish I could swing that way—it's not like I'll get any beauty tips from a 230-pound rugby player. If I found someone my own size, I could double my wardrobe, though I wouldn't be caught dead wearing plaid.

I'm having a great time sitting here taking in the scene and wondering if I could actually get a chick that hot. After three beers and two waters, I decide the end of the evening has come and I leave as inconspicuously as I entered. The heat of the outdoors feels delicious on my skin after a few hours of air conditioning and so many years of freezing my ass off in the Northeast.

Driving down the highway with the lights of Vegas to my right and Henderson in front of me, I turn on the radio of my eight-year-old Saturn. Although I've heard the tune a thousand million times before in various stages of my life, for the first time, Steppenwolf's "Born to Be Wild" is actually kicking in.

I realize I can't have a night out like this when he comes back. I can't say one minute I want with all my heart for him to stop drinking and then say let's go out on the town. If he wasn't able to keep it together in Utah, where there were no temptations and not a goddamn thing to do at night, how can he ever make it in Las Vegas? I suppose we wouldn't have to go to bars. We can go to the library and to movies and out to eat and take in yoga classes and go to our support group meetings.

Yeah, that seems like a blast. That's what Vegas is all about. We might as well move back to Mormonland.

2.

Yesterday I signed up to be a hospice volunteer, something I did for a few years back in Albany after Chris and I split up. This will be good. I've spent far too many days in anger this summer, and hanging out with dying people might be just the thing to cheer me up.

I became familiar with the hospice program when Granny, my maternal grandmother, had home hospice care after breast cancer progressed into her bones. I have to admit that as a kid, Granny wasn't my favorite grandmother. In contrast to my dear Nana, who indulged us to no end, Granny was more the "don't touch that, dear" type, a clean freak who'd set the table with the plates face down so they wouldn't gather dust before dinnertime and who stored her Electrolux in a plastic bag to maintain its hygienic state while it wasn't in use. As I got older and recognized some of Granny's neuroses in myself, I came to appreciate her more, and when I became a grandmother, I decided my grandson should call me Granny, too, since I'm simply not agreeable enough to be a Nana. (Of course, in public I prefer to be called Aunt Linda.)

Through the hospice program, Granny got all her drugs, her durable medical equipment, and Rob, her home health aide. A cuddly gay man a few years younger than me, Rob took care of Granny and did her cooking, cleaning, shopping, and laundry from 6 p.m.

Sunday until 6 p.m. Friday, with my mother and aunts rotating coverage on the weekends. Granny liked Rob, a fact that prompted a collective sigh of relief through the family since none of the aides who had come and gone before him could meet her uncompromising standards.

A six-month prognosis is the prerequisite for receiving hospice services. Granny lasted over two years. Until almost the very end, she ran her household from the hospital bed in her room, directing Rob as he did his chores under her watchful eye. "No, dear," she'd tell him, "fold that lengthwise first…No, lengthwise…Here, give it to me." She'd then demonstrate the proper technique—origami for bath towels—implying that Rob's closet at home was nothing but a ruinous mess of linens. And though she hadn't actually made it to the kitchen in months, there'd be hell to pay if she found out the blue dish towel with the rooster on it wasn't, in fact, in the second drawer on the left side of the dishwasher. If I were Rob, I'd have been into Granny's liquid morphine every chance I could.

The role of granddaughter, however, afforded me special status and a few degrees of separation from the Medicare discrepancies, estate details, and other irritations that my mother and aunts had to contend with. Granny didn't always seem to appreciate the demands of those responsibilities, and in the same way that I could do nothing wrong, often they could do nothing right. They found ways to take revenge, like the day I walked in and caught them all jumping on Granny's living room furniture.

"Shhh…" My mother giggled as she pressed her index finger to her lips.

"I'm telling," I deadpanned, and headed for Granny's bedroom.

I looked forward to our visits. "Hi, Gran!" I'd sing, in a voice channeled from seventh grade. There she'd sit, propped up in her satin bed jacket and sunglasses, dragging on a cigarette through freshly manicured fingernails like a 1940s film star.

Granny enjoyed hearing the details of my life, and to her I'd offer the unedited version, revealing as much as I would to one of my girlfriends. Vicariously she attended grad school, drove children to dance and music lessons, and went out to hear reggae bands. Often she'd ask about my plans for the evening and before I could finish, she'd reach for the pocketbook slung on the side rail of her bed, a summer bag she no longer changed with the seasons. "Here, take this," she'd command, pressing a twenty into my palm.

"No, Gran. I don't need any money," I'd say, lying to my grandmother on her deathbed.

I loved to get her going on the subject of weight. Granny was always a bit plump before she got sick, so once she dipped under a hundred pounds, she cashed right in on that superior edge our society affords to thin people. Everyone was getting *so fat*—Mom, my aunts, Rob, Oprah. "The other day, your mother bent over, and honest to God, her ass is this big," she told me, extending two bony arms. "But dear, you're just right. Here, have a nice praline."

Before leaving, I would always make sure to ask Granny if she needed anything at the store, praying the answer would be "no." Although I would have done anything for her, I feared running into someone from high school, or worse, having a cute guy in back of me at the checkout line while I'm purchasing Depends, laxatives, the *National Enquirer*, and a carton of Virginia Slims.

Granny died in 1993, shortly before her eighty-first birthday. For some people, the final chapter of life may be the best. In a way, Granny never had it better than in her last days, with her bags of Pepperidge Farm cookies, stacks of celebrity tabloids, and a gentle gay man to do her hair and nails. I've never felt sorry for hospice patients; whereas most of us have no idea when our time will be up, they can pretty much narrow it down. And while we might be found splattered across the pavement in a frantic staging of flashing red lights, hospice patients are virtually guaranteed to die quietly, either in their own bed or in the serenity of the inpatient unit, surrounded by their family and a loving medical staff. Really, it's the way to go.

My marriage to Chris ended soon after Granny passed. A year later I became a hospice volunteer, having decided I'd prefer to share my life not with another man, but with other feisty old broads like Granny.

The first patient they assigned to me was a sweet little lady who, quite honestly, seemed perfectly healthy. We hit it off right away. Every Saturday morning I'd take Chickie to her favorite coffee shop for breakfast, then afterward we'd visit a while longer in her two-room, government-subsidized senior apartment. The place reminded me of a college dormitory, with its common lounge area, entertainment schedule, and half the residents wandering around all doped up. Sometimes Chickie's eighty-six-year-old Avon lady would drop by. While I browsed through the monthly beauty specials, the two of them would gossip about how Alice Feeney so shamelessly throws herself at Harold Van Pelt, one of the few single men in the building.

The volunteer coordinator at the hospice here in Vegas told me we're not allowed to take patients out of their homes. I guess families were complaining about their inheritances being blown at the casinos. That's too bad. Chickie would never have gotten out if it weren't for me.

The day I met her she was all dolled up, ready for me to take her to the DMV. She'd given up her seventeen-year-old Mercury Comet a few months before, but it was important to Chickie to keep her license current. I laugh when I think of her twirling aimlessly in front of the blue screen as the clerk tried to take her picture. "No, over here... This way...No, no, face me...Okay, that's it...Don't move now." The guy was patient enough, but if it takes someone twenty minutes to stand on a piece of masking tape, is it really a good idea to let her operate a motor vehicle? Considering the five-year renewal period and Chickie's status as a hospice patient, I wanted to take him aside to see if I could negotiate a special short-term rate.

Chickie had the last laugh. She lived almost until her license was up for renewal again and eventually was discharged from the hospice program, since evidently she wasn't dying after all. "Do you know they thought I had only six months to live?" she asked me. I admitted my awareness of that fact, and thought that although it would have been nice for her doctors to clue her in, sometimes it's best not to know what other people are scheming up for you.

Chickie and I were together three years. It's pretty bad when your relationship with a hospice patient lasts longer than your marriage.

3.

Bastard Husband is arriving this afternoon at 2:47. Sometimes I'm
not sure if I want to fire things up with him again or not. I've had
two and a half months of freedom from asshole-y behavior. It's been
nice—no worrying about an incidental remark turning into a three-
day argument, no eggshells to tread ever-so-carefully upon. I don't
miss living in that constant state of apprehension waiting for the
other shoe to drop. Then again, I know what a mess I'd be if he said
he planned to stay in New Zealand for good.

So what *are* his plans?

I want to look hot when he sees me. Not that I've ever had to
worry about that—he's always been complimentary about my appearance. "You look good, babe," he'd say, never once qualifying the
sentiment by adding, "for your age." And he's never said a word
about my crappy hair—it's like he doesn't even notice it. I kind of
feel I've been pulling something over on him all this time, and if
he really took a good look at me, he'd recoil in horror. Please, God,
let things work out with us. I don't have the self-esteem to break in
a new guy.

I've always liked his looks, too, as perpetually disheveled as they
are, and find his extra weight a bit comforting. God knows I'm not
secure enough to be with someone thinner than I am. Even when

I found his actions reprehensible, I could still look at him and see nothing but perfection; the attraction defies logic. Chemistry overrides everything with me, and considering his body chemistry is precisely what's totally out of whack, I have to wonder which one of us is more screwed up.

Before I leave to pick him up, I check myself one last time in the full-length mirror in the bedroom. I do look good. This cute little spaghetti-strap top I bought yesterday goes well with the black miniskirt I wore to Boulder Station last week. I'm nice and tan— even my legs—from hanging out at the pool every day. Sometimes I worry about getting wrinkles or skin cancer from the sun, but the fact is, a tan makes you feel twenty pounds thinner and if you ask me, that's worth the risk.

Hmmmm...I'd better see what the lighting in the bathroom does. I once saw an Oprah episode about people who "get lost" in the mirror and can't pull themselves away. I can totally understand that—you can always find one more flaw to scrutinize. The sad part is, no matter how many times you've gone over every cell of your face in the house, there's sure to be some undetected horror that's revealed only by your car's rear view mirror.

§ § §

The Arrivals board says his flight just landed. Perfect timing. I walk along the row of slot machines that bisects the baggage claim area. They ding-ding-ding while videos promoting shows on the Strip blare from the giant screens perched above all the madness. A morbidly obese man who hasn't shaved in a month glumly pokes away at a Lucky Seven machine. Red pants with a red t-shirt...looks like Santa's hit hard times. The message on his chest says, "I have nothing nice to say." No wonder he's not winning. What kind of karma do you create for yourself by sending that sentiment out to the world?

People start to gather around the baggage carousel. He'll be one of the last ones here from his flight, I guarantee. Besides the fact that he's never in a hurry, most likely he'll leave something on the plane and have to go back for it.

Everybody looks happy to have landed in Vegas, glowing with anticipation of the debauchery ahead. What will his face look like? On some level, he must be a little anxious about returning. He can't feel good about what's happened between us.

A young couple embraces as they await their luggage. What will our reunion be like? Will he have the same heartfelt emotion as when I dropped him off two and a half months ago—none? He probably dreads coming back to the ball-and-chain, the killjoy I've become. He sure as hell hasn't said he's coming back because he misses me or that he's given up drinking and looks forward to a new life of sobriety.

I want things to go well. They might not. Really, they might not. I don't know what to expect. We talked briefly the other night, but only about the logistics of his flight. Why didn't I ask him just what the hell he has planned for our relationship? Are we going to be in love again and take our road trips and do our yoga and work on the *USA Today* crosswords together? Or does he expect to drink and gamble all night and use our apartment as a flophouse?

My neck is starting to blotch. I should be more positive.

I bet he won't have his wedding ring on. He probably took it off in New Zealand and lost it. He loses everything. He doesn't do well by himself.

Oh, there he is on the other side of the carousel. He doesn't see me. Why isn't he wearing his glasses? Lost, I bet. He looks, well, like someone who's been traveling for twenty-four straight hours. I approach him from the side.

"Hi."

"Oh, hi." I seem to have taken him by surprise, as if he's not quite ready to see me.

"How was your flight?"

"It was good. I had the whole row to myself coming over."

"That's good."

He smoothes his hair. Though the motion does nothing to control the unruly mop, it allows me to see he's wearing his ring. *Yes!*

"How was your connection from LA?" I ask, with a boost of spirit.

"It was fine. Yeah."

We stand side by side watching baggage tumble onto the conveyor.

"You'd better give me a proper hello," I finally say. He offers an obligatory hug, with nothing behind it.

So this is how it's going to be.

The mid-day traffic is heavy on the way home. *Ask him*, the voice of reason urges me. *Ask him just what the hell his intentions are.*

"Are you hungry?" I say.

Oh, for Christsake! Tell him you're not taking any more of his bullshit. Tell him he can live with you only if he'll stop drinking and gambling and start being a good husband. Tell him!

"I bought some nice salmon this morning."

You fucking idiot.

§ § §

Although I super-cleaned the apartment last night, it's a mess within moments. He rummages through the chaos in the larger of his two big bags, and then opens the other one, which is equally well-organized. There's no need to fold clothes when you're going for that "just out of the blender" look.

"Here," he says, presenting me with a paper bag. "I got this for you when I went to the south island."

I take it and pull out a beautiful purple and blue fleece jacket.

"Wow! This is really nice." I can't hide my amazement. Historically, he's been "challenged" when it comes to gift giving.

I put it on and follow the well-worn path to the full length mirror. I look funny wearing a winter jacket over summer clothes. "It fits perfectly. Thank you!"

"There's something in the pocket, eh."

A little bag holds a delicate paua shell necklace. "This is beautiful! Thanks." I'm shocked.

He smiles for the first time since we've seen each other. "There's something in the other pocket, too."

I hope you know CPR, I want to say. I reach in and pull out another little bag. It's a pair of earrings. They go well with the necklace.

"This is so nice. Thank you, thank you so much." We hug tightly and I remember how good it feels to sink into his sweaty embrace. Maybe things will be different this time.

"Are you hungry?" I ask. "I can cook up that salmon."

4.

The plan was for him to go up to school in Utah on Mondays and return Thursday nights. That was the plan, although only once in the past three weeks has he actually made it home on a Thursday night. It's now Friday morning, going for eleven o'clock. He rolled in twenty minutes ago all full of himself with a fistful of hundred dollar bills. Amazing how he always wins. His grand entrance was met with silence.

I don't know where he's been and I don't care. I had a good sleep last night, that's what matters to me. I didn't miss him waking me at 3:30, bragging about how everyone thinks he's the greatest guy. *I* think you're the greatest guy, I used to tell him. My validation didn't matter.

Now he's passed out, snoring like a water bong in the bed I made up once already today. Halted breaths punctuate the gurgling, a familiar resonance. Sometimes when I lie beside him, I count those moments of emptiness. Eventually I nudge him and he resumes the serenade with an extra loud snort, a sound that is either repulsive or reassuring, depending on how I feel about him at the moment.

Standing in the bedroom doorway, I watch him struggle to complete each breath. I bet I could press a pillow into his face and no one would know the difference.

I'm getting out of here. I collect my towel, sunscreen and hat, and stop at the bookcase in search of the spiritual tome that will give me the strength to get through another fucking day. I select a classic, Louise Hay's *You Can Heal Your Life.*

In the seconds before I leave, I'm inspired to turn on the TV, just a few feet away from the mess in the bed. Perfect—it's *The View.* I was hoping for Oprah, but this is even better. I press the volume button seven times and slip out the front door.

The pool's been quiet lately, since the kids are now back in school, and this morning I especially welcome the solitude. I'm not up to exchanging pleasantries with the neighbors today, as nice as some of them are. Basking in the mid-September sun, I think how lucky I am to be lying poolside this time of year. People are already wearing sweaters back in Albany.

I open my book, close my eyes, and randomly select a page. When you do this, you're supposed to be divinely guided to the exact message you need to hear right now. I open my eyes and am drawn to a line already marked by my highlighter.

Each of us is doing the very best we can at this very moment.

I ponder the sentiment for a minute or two and conclude that's a load of shit. There's no way he's doing the best he can. I'm sorry, but sometimes people are just lazy. Everyone can try a little harder. I see that in yoga. You can always stretch a tenth of an inch more or go into a posture a tenth of an inch deeper. You can always put forth a little more effort. I love my spiritual books, but sometimes they piss me off.

No more reading. I want to sit here and stew.

I should throw him out. I bet I could. I'm strong these days, and I'm no longer stranded in the middle of the prairie, or in the middle of goddamn Mormonland. I like it here. I know my way around. I have friends. Well, one friend, but I'll make more. I'll find a job, too.

It hasn't all been horrible since he's been back. I took him to the Railhead the one Thursday night he did make it home. The band wasn't great, but I ran into that guy Dan, from the DMV, and Frank, the dapper black man who's always after me to dance. I felt good introducing him to them. I was like, "Look! I know people! I've found cool stuff to do! I have a life without you!" Of some sort.

And he did agree to go to church with me last Sunday, which was nice. I've been going back to that metaphysical place in the crazy shopping plaza almost every week. As the two of us sat on the folding chairs in the back of the sanctuary, I felt overwhelmed with gratitude to have him beside me. And when the gentle chimes signaled the beginning of the meditation period, I prayed in earnest. *Thank you for bringing him back to me*, I started. *Please surround him with your love and give him the strength to overcome his struggles. And...Jesus Christ, is he asleep?* A sly glance to my left confirmed my suspicion. I watched his head bob rhythmically until he startled himself back to awareness.

"Oh...Sorry, babe," he whispered with a guilty smile.

On the way home I asked, "So, what did you think?"

"That little nap felt good, eh."

"I mean about the sermon."

"Oh. The old guy's a good speaker," he said, referring to the minister, or pastor, or whatever the hell he is.

"Yeah, I always get something out of it."

After a while, he murmured, "I don't think I'm a God person."

"Well, I don't know if I'd call myself a God person, either," I responded, "but..." I trailed off. The sentence wasn't worth finishing.

We rode in silence, and I realized I feel lonelier in his presence than I do when I'm by myself. I spent an entire summer praying for him and sending him positive healing vibrations and for what? It's like I've taken up a perverse hobby that fucks with my sanity.

I don't think I'm a God person. His declaration hurt my heart. It's clear his spirit has left him, the demons are in full control. No surprise—there's been nothing behind his eyes for ages.

Where is the charming man who celebrated the cosmicness of the universe with me in Niagara Falls? And where is the spirit of his father now? Why doesn't Michael McNeil give him some kind of sign to straighten his sorry ass out?

§ § §

Bastard Husband enters the pool area and joins me in the hot tub.

"I'm surprised to see you," I say.

"Those screaming yentas woke me up. I couldn't get back to sleep."

"Oh, did I leave the TV on? Sorry."

A young couple plays in the water, drinking Coors Lights from the side of the pool, she in an aqua bikini that shows off her perfect body, he in his tattoos. I catch myself rolling my eyes at her flirtatious giggle; Louise Hay would scold me for being judgmental. Someday they'll discover the dark side in each other that's sure to surface with time and familiarity. Good.

"Did you submit that paper?" I ask. During the week I offered to edit an article he'd written for his department's newsletter. I spent quite some time on it, and felt pleased with the results.

"Yeah. I sent it in yesterday."

"You must be glad to have that off your plate."

"Yeah."

I'm waiting.

I'm waiting.

Sometimes I fucking hate him.

"What you mean to say is 'thanks for all your help,' right?"

"Oh, yeah. Thanks. You did a good job."

"Right."

The words I couldn't say on the way home from the airport last month come back to me now. I can no longer store those words in my head; the pressure is too much to bear. Finally my mouth expels them like my brain is spitting up.

"You need to get help, or get out." *There.*

He closes his eyes and turns his face to the sun like a basking vacationer.

I'm waiting.

I'm waiting.

"Do I have to decide right now?" he finally asks.

"I can't live with this bullshit."

"So do I have to decide right now?"

Don't get snotty with me, you prick.

"By the time you leave for school on Monday," I answer, my composure amazingly intact.

"Okay, then." His eyebrow twitches, as it does when he's nervous.

Sometimes I remember to try to look at him through the eyes of love. I can't do that right now.

Okay, that's over. "Are we still going out tonight?" I ask.

"Sure. You want to see that movie, right?"

"Yeah. Denis Leary's in it."

"You like him, eh."

"*Like* him?" Is he kidding? "I want to tie him up and fuck him stupid!" I grin dementedly, thrilled to remember the sensation, however entrenched in fantasy, that's lain dormant for all too long: passion.

§ § §

"I could have done without all the vomiting," he says as we walk through the parking lot.

"No kidding," I reply. The family in the movie, *The Secret Lives of Dentists*, had the flu and somebody puked in nearly every scene.

"And all the closeups of dental work, eh. Why did they have to show that?"

"Denis Leary was good." I unlock the passenger door and hold it open for him, knowing full well I annoy him when I do that. He thinks it's emasculating, but tonight he makes no comment.

"I'm not feeling well," he tells me as I start up the car.

I shoot him a look. "You haven't slept much lately." What the hell do you expect?

"I think I need to go to the emergency room."

As I process his words, the bitchiness and resentment I've been holding transform into concern. "What do you mean? What's going on?" The car turns itself onto West Sahara, the way it came in.

"I feel like I'm having a heart attack."

"Okay," I say with a different composure from when we sat at the pool this afternoon. That was confident composure. Now I'm faking it.

"Do you know where there's a hospital?" His voice sounds weak.

"Not really. Not out here." We're on the extreme western edge of Las Vegas. "I know there's one near our apartment. It's on Lake Mead Boulevard, across from Hotdog Heaven."

"Drive there, then."

"It's far. We're over twenty miles away."

"Drive there."

I speed east on the 215 toward Henderson. The silence enveloping the car is a different silence from what hung between us at the pool.

"Are you alright?" I ask, placing my hand on his leg.

"Yeah." He seems to breathe deliberately.

My mind races faster than the car. I can't believe this, though I've had a feeling that sooner or later this day would come. He's overweight, he hasn't been to a doctor since...not since I've known him. God knows what his blood pressure's like. His father died of a heart attack. At 52. *No, no! He's only 38. Don't take him from me.*

I won't ask again if he's okay. I want to, but I don't want to risk annoying him.

"I'm feeling a little better," he reports, answering my unvoiced query.

"That's good, honey." *Thank you, God.*

"I've been eating too many carbohydrates lately."

Yeah, that's what's doing it. Carbohydrates.

"On the plane coming back from New Zealand, I thought of all the things I want to do before I die. I'm not ready."

I don't want to hear that kind of talk. "You're feeling better now, right?"

"A little better."

"You still want to go to the emergency room?"

"I think I should."

§ § §

He is well enough to give his personal information to the intake clerk.

"Married?" she asks.

"Yes."

She looks up at me over her half glasses and then back at him. After collecting the details of his insurance coverage, she directs him to the triage nurse through the double doors.

"Can my wife go in with me?" he wants to know.

He's married, and he wants his wife to be with him. This is great.

5.

"He's out," I inform the circle of faces in my Tuesday night divorce group. "I threw him out yesterday morning. I told him, 'When you go up to school today, take your sh-sh-crap with you. And don't think you're coming back here Thursday night.'" My heart pounds as I relay my declaration.

Everyone's eyes shift between me and Chuck, our facilitator, the guy who hangs the Absolutely No Swearing sign from the ceiling every week.

"So you're in a different place with him than you were last week," Chuck says in that annoying voice I've heard therapists use when they're "reflecting back" the obvious.

I realize I'm glaring at him, my anger misdirected. And Chuck is not a therapist, he's a regular guy who's been running this group for twenty-four years out of the goodness of his heart. I'm sure I'm not the first person who's sat here ready to kill someone. Chuck must know he's not my target.

"You were concerned about him," he continues. "He had a health scare, am I remembering correctly?"

"Yeah. It wasn't a heart attack, though. They don't know what happened. He had tests last Friday. I guess they'll call with the results."

As Chuck and the others wait for more, I assess the scribbles on the wall drawn by the children whose preschool room we're borrowing. Pedro's the most talented artist, if you ask me. I think of how the nasty details of adult life spill into a space that houses the innocence of preschoolers by day. I hope Chuck cleanses the energy after we leave to prevent this negativity from infecting the kids.

"Do you want to tell us what happened?" he asks.

No, I don't, Chuck. I don't want to sit in this stupid fucking group at all.

"I've had enough of his crap," I answer. I continue to nod for a few seconds in lieu of "sharing" my Sunday night discovery. I've put up with a lot, but some things I will not tolerate. I can't bring myself to verbalize them right now. "It's for the best," I conclude.

Yeah, it's all good.

§ § §

I'm sitting at the bedside of a woman who may or may not be dead. I can't tell if she's still breathing. Her face holds not the slightest bit of tension, her mouth so relaxed it droops open a crack. I take her hand and notice the remnants of cherry red nail polish from a not-too recent manicure. She feels neither warm nor cool.

I know nothing about this lady except her name is Helen. Some hospice patients have family pictures or mementos displayed that clue you in to who they are, or who they used to be, as well as the people who care about them. A bouquet that was fresh a couple of days ago sits on the table next to the window. There's no card, though, so that's nothing to go by. Sometimes when patients die, the family donates flowers from the funeral, which we rearrange in vases so they're not obvious reminders of someone's passing. I haven't noticed any visitors in Helen's room, but maybe people were here when I wasn't. I hope so, but where are they now?

Helen's not scary or anything. She looks like if she woke up, she'd be nice. I like sitting with her.

A nurse comes in to check on my silent friend. Jerry's a burly man with such a baby face I bet I could pick him out of his kindergarten class picture.

He stands next to me, hands on his hips. "She's still hanging in there, huh?"

"I guess so." How can he tell just by looking at her? I'd feel more assured if he placed two fingers on her jugular.

Jerry drops one hand and delivers a couple of firm pats to my shoulder. "Happy Birthday, by the way."

"Thanks." Someone from the day shift must have told him it's my birthday. I can still feel the echo of his touch.

"Any big plans?" he asks.

I motion toward Helen. "This is it. Another swinging Friday night in Vegas." We both laugh and he leaves the room shaking his head. "There's still some cake left," I call after him. "Help yourself!"

The volunteer coordinator brought in a cake for me and had the whole staff sign one of those generic cards you buy for someone you don't really know. That was nice of her. I'm forty-six now, half the age of the dying body I'm keeping company.

Several more birthday wishes await me at home, no doubt, but I can't deal with anyone today, no matter how well-meaning. No one can get at me here. That's good. Although now I'll have to call everyone back tomorrow, and that'll be worse. I got a message Tuesday night after my group meeting. He's coming by Saturday morning to get the rest of his things. Fuck.

"Oh, Helen…" I sigh. At least one of us will be out of our misery soon.

Some people talk to patients when death is imminent, believing they can hear right to the very end. That may be true, but I won't put Helen through that—the poor soul would probably rush toward the light. Listening to my seething rant is no way to spend your last minutes on earth, that's for sure.

Not everyone here in the inpatient unit hangs at the edge of life, like Helen. Some patients have a temporary setback and simply need a few days of TLC from the nursing staff. Then they'll go back home. A few are here for respite, to give their caregivers a break. These people are sometimes ambulatory and they don't have to stay in their pajamas all day if they're up for getting dressed. I often sit with them in the courtyard while they have a cigarette, since they can't smoke in the rooms. A lot of hospice patients smoke, I've noticed. At this point, what the hell.

Back in Albany, I was a home-care volunteer, which meant the hospice assigned me to people like Granny, who received services in their homes. Unlike this place, which is a free-standing facility, the inpatient unit in Albany occupied a wing in one of the hospitals. I didn't spend much time there, only when my home-care patients were near the end.

One afternoon, a nurse called to tell me I'd better come in to say good-bye to one of my ladies who had taken a turn. Aunt Marie, as we called her, was a big, black Mabel King-type-of mama with eyes that bugged with intensity. I would visit her every Sunday afternoon and do her laundry or pick up her apartment—the very chores I put off doing in my own house. Marie acknowledged my every effort with a "thank you, baby" or "bless your heart, child," which made it all worth it.

I sat with Marie in the hospice for hours and hours the day I got that call, listening to soft gospel music while she drifted in and out of wakefulness. Eventually it came time for me to go home.

I bent over and kissed her cheek, thankful she had made it that far into the night. "Good-bye, Aunt Marie." I said, supposing it would be the last time I'd ever see her.

"Good-bye, baby," she replied, in nearly a whisper.

"I love you, Aunt Marie." I sure did.

"I love you, too, baby."

On my way to the door, I heard a faint voice ask, "Are you gaining weight in your behind?"

It was a classic Three Stooges, *Slowly I turn...*" moment. "What was that, Marie?"

She smiled and nodded, and with more strength than she'd managed all day, repeated her words. "Are you gaining weight in your behind, baby?"

"Um, I don't think so." I gave her a puzzled look. "I'll be back tomorrow." *And you'd better be alive and conversing because those will NOT be your last words to me.*

How I would love to be able to put my head in Aunt Marie's lap right now and have her stroke my hair.

It's after 9 p.m. Before I leave Helen, I silently thank her for the peace she's brought me this evening and for the privilege of sitting in her presence. Since it's safe to say she's already spoken her last words, I don't have to back out of the room.

§ § §

"Are you ready to open your present?" he asked.

It was my forty-third birthday, the first event in our relationship that involved a gift.

"Here," said my beloved, smiling like a little kid with a hand-made present for his Mum. "I wrapped it myself, eh. I bought the paper at Walgreens and everything. It's the first one I ever wrapped."

"You're kidding!" I blurted, disbelief mingling with heartfelt sympathy for his former girlfriends.

I sat at the foot of the bed and eyed the package, imagining his taste in trinkets. I know a box with a necklace in it when I see one, I thought. He beamed as he watched me open his gift. A hundred tiny slips of paper lay where my necklace was supposed to be.

"Wow...what is this?" I asked.

"They're coupons, babe. Look, they have points." He sat next to me and practically caressed them.

"Oh..." I took a closer look, maintaining a bemused smile. "What's that they say? Marlboro?" *What the hell...???*

"Yeah, they come with my cigarettes. I've been saving these up for months." He positively glowed. "I had to smoke a lot to get all these points!"

"I bet."

"And now I'm giving them to you. Look," he said, presenting me with some kind of booklet, "you can trade the points in for stuff. See, you can get an umbrella or a sweatshirt or whatever you want."

"Oh, yeah . . . and, um, they all say 'Marlboro' on them, too." *Where the hell is my necklace?*

"Babe, don't you get it? This is the greatest present! I'm giving my points away because I quit smoking. That's a great present, right? You want me to quit smoking, right?"

"Yes, of course, I do," I said, believing that surely my real gift would still surface.

I spent three birthdays with him, and the fourteen thousand Marlboro points, which I never did redeem, actually turned out to be the best present of the lot. We were living in Laramie the day I turned forty-four. He ran out early that morning and returned twenty minutes later with a Wyoming coffee mug he no doubt picked up at the 7-Eleven, along with a pack of cigarettes. Last year, a few days before my birthday, he simply turned to me in Target and said, "Why don't you pick something out and it can be your present from me?"

Dammit! Why didn't I wait another week to throw him out? He's probably earned a ton of player points from the Station casinos by now. I could be unwrapping a new windbreaker.

The truth is, though, he gave me anything I wanted. I lacked for nothing. And it didn't have to be my birthday.

§ § §

On the way home from the hospice I decide to treat myself and stop for a six-pack of Sierra Nevada porter and an *Us* magazine. Now that's a present.

As expected, my machine blinks with messages from Mom, my sister Lori, my sister Stacie, my friend Jerry in New Orleans, my sister Lisa, and my nutty friend Little Betsy in Colorado. I'll call her back. She won't bum me out.

First I scan the list of new emails. Yippee! There's one from Bob, one of the instructional designers I worked with at GE. I can't believe he remembered my birthday. I'll read these later—something to look forward to. I'd better call Betsy before it gets too late.

Little Betsy is what my grandmother would call a "kook." She's one of those marathon runners with an uber-metabolism and six kids ranging from twenty-one to five. Barely tipping a hundred pounds, Betsy once loaded her pockets with rolls of quarters so she'd weigh enough to give blood. She means well. Though we've seen each other only a handful of times since our college days in Plattsburgh, I hear from her every October 3 without fail.

"Hi, Bets. It's Linda," I start off.

"Heeeeey! Happy Birthday! I've been thinking about you all day!" Betsy's voice marks every sentence with an exclamation point.

"Thanks. How's it going?"

She jumps right in. "Oh-my-God! You are *NOT* gonna believe this! Hold on, let me get a beer. Are you having a beer? Let's have a beer together! It's your birthday!"

"Yeah, I opened one a minute ago." Already I'm delighted I returned her call, though I won't get three words in the whole conversation. I relax on the couch and get ready for the ride. "So what's going on? Don't tell me you're pregnant again."

"No! Omigod—ha! No!" Her tone lowers for dramatic effect. "Check this out…I'm having surgery. I've got, like, wicked hemorrhoids."

"Oh, my God! That's awful!" Now I'm the one with the vocal exclamation points.

"Yeah, from all the babies. Oh, but they're worth it! I love my babies!"

She *is* a kook.

"That's not all…" she continues. Of course, that's not all. Betsy's voice again deepens as she leads me to the next level of disclosure. "Plus, like, if I'm running a long race, sometimes, omigod…this is gross . . . I can't control my shit. It's *dis-gust-ing*!" She whines the last word.

I don't know how to respond. I've heard that marathon runners can sometimes leave a trail of crap behind them. "So, what do you mean? Does it, like, seep down your leg?"

"Oh, no, it's not that bad—oh my God, no—but the worst part is they have to do two separate surgeries. I'm like, *pull-eeze*, can't you take care of everything at once while you're down there?" She giggles, then asks, "So how are things with you?"

How do I compete with that?

"Um…well…I've had asshole problems, too, but I threw him out Monday morning."

"HA-ha-ha-ha!" Betsy loves that one. "It's about time!"

"I've taken a lot of his crap, but there are some things I will not put up with. Last Sunday night..."

"Whatever you do, don't take him back," she interrupts. "I mean it. Even if he stops drinking, he'll only get addicted to those stupid recovery meetings. That's what happened to Arnie—he traded one addiction for another. You don't need that."

Betsy's ex-husband was an alcoholic, so whatever I have to say is old news. She's back to relaying every detail of her recent colonoscopy and appointments with various ass doctors. Just as well; I'd rather listen to her shit than talk about mine.

An hour and a half later we say goodbye. She's outdone herself this time, and has elevated my mood a hundred-fold. There's nothing like someone else's hemorrhoids and fecal incontinence to entertain you on your birthday.

Little Betsy is the greatest friend.

§ § §

My emails! I'll sit and finish this beer first. I still can't believe Bob remembered my birthday.

Oh, I *love* Bob! I love all the friends I made at GE. There were five of us—me, three other women, and our darling Bob—in our naughty little group. We lived for our lunch hour, which typically digressed into sixty minutes of debauchery. After toiling all morning in Six Sigma process improvement, we'd bust out of our work cubicles at the stroke of noon and settle into a corner of the cafeteria, far from the more self-controlled workforce professionals.

Bob usually set our daily agenda items, many culled from the Howard Stern show. One day we figured out our porn star names. You do this by combining the name of your childhood pet with the name of the street you grew up on. If I were a porn star, I'd be Ginger Lincoln.

And we had great fun with the "If you had to be gay," question, which meant if you had to be gay but could have your choice of any celebrity, who would you pick for yourself? (My choice: Beverly D'Angelo.) "The Question" so fascinated me, I started to incorporate it into my nightly chitchat in the hotel lounge and even used it as a screening mechanism for dating. If anyone refused to play along, I'd say I couldn't possibly go out with someone so homophobic.

A good-looking guy resembling John Travolta, Bob loved to hold court with stories of his rambunctious youth and extended adolescence. By his own admission, he could have easily amounted to little more than an incorrigible stoner, but by his late forties he somehow found himself in a life that included a gorgeous wife, two beautiful little kids, a house in Connecticut, and a decent income from a world-class conglomerate.

"When I was a kid on Long Island," he started one noontime off, in his signature deliberate manner, "during the summer I mowed lawns at a cemetery." He paused to savor the attention from his adoring harem. "And one day, I'm mowing along and I come across a grave that says 'Hiscock.' That was the guy's name."

We tittered with anticipation of the story unraveling into something bawdy.

"And underneath his name," he continued, "there under 'Hiscock,' it says—I swear, this is true—'In God's Hands.'" With that, Bob crossed his arms and sat back, pleased with his ability to make us roar like prepubescent boys.

I finish my porter and read through my birthday greetings, saving Bob's for last. Finally I click on his message.

Bob did not remember my birthday—the correspondence is directed to the four of us girls.

"I hate to lay this on you, but yesterday I got con-firmation that I have a cancerous tumor in one of my lymph nodes. It's a secondary tumor, which means there's a primary somewhere else. They don't know. Next week I'm having tests to see if they can find out what's going on. Wendy and I are staying positive. All I ask is that no one puts me in the Ghoul Pool."

The Ghoul Pool—our contest where we each came up with a list of the most sickly, frail, or reckless public figures we identified as most likely to kick. We must have blown an entire week of productivity on that one.

Bob's news shakes me into sobriety. I scrutinize his words, searching for the joke. What happened on Howard today? There has to be a tie-in somewhere. I turn off the computer, open yet another beer in an attempt to restore the buzz, and plant myself back on the couch.

It's 12:02 on the cable box—not my birthday anymore. Bastard Husband will be here in ten hours to pick up the rest of his crap. I close my eyes and through the slight inebriation, send positive vibes into the next morning. I give thanks that I'm not lying in a hospice, I have no god-awful bowel problems, and nobody's told me there's cancer lurking somewhere in my body.

So I have a bastard husband. Big deal.

6.

"Do you want this glass from the brew pub in New Mexico?" he asks, staring into the kitchen cabinets.

"Take it."

He combs through the apartment, opening drawers and closet doors in one last search for stray possessions while I sit at the table and pretend to read the newspaper. I watch with a furtive eye to make sure he doesn't dare lift anything of mine.

What's he doing over by the CDs? He went through them last spring before he left for New Zealand. I jump up.

"That's my Lucinda Williams. You already took yours," I snap, referring to one of the very few duplicate discs we purchased independently before we met. "Here's a Black Sabbath. You can take that."

"Yeah, I guess I can, since it's mine," he retorts.

I hate him. I hate him with every molecule in my body. At least this should be the last time I'll ever have to look at his stupid fucking face.

I never should have taken him back. God knows we've been in the relationship hospice for how long and this marriage was not coming back to life. After what I came across last Sunday night, it's my turn to hold the remote, and for once he's forced to react to *my* decision. It's about time. I've always had to react to him, my happiness always hinging on his terms.

He leaves to take another armful of clothes to the car.

How did it ever come to this? How do you go from being the love of someone's life to a detested enemy? How can I despise him so, yet bemoan what are sure to be our final moments in each other's presence?

I wonder how his appointment with the cardiologist went yesterday. I won't ask; I won't give the impression I care. Jesus, only two weeks ago I sat at his bedside playing the role of patient advocate, tracking down doctors and test results and bitching at the poor staff workers.

For once we were on the same team, allies against the evil medical bureaucracy. It was the closest we'd been in ages. I loved it.

Mona said whatever you do, don't cry in front of him. I'm not going to. I've been very good trying to match his robotic facade.

"I think that's it," he says, returning red and sweaty from the exertion. I look up from the paper.

"How do you want to handle the car?" he wants to know. I'm supposed to get his Saturn, according to the divorce agreement, but haven't made an issue of it, in case things worked out.

"I don't know." My face starts to hold tension, as it does when I want to cry.

"It's easiest if I just buy it from you, right? Do you want me to write you a check?"

"Whatever." I can't tell if anger is fueling the sadness or vice versa. "I want three thousand," I tell him. It's worth about two.

He pauses to assess my offer. Opting not to contest it, he sits across the table from me and makes out the check. His left ring finger is bare, and that observation breaks the dam that's been welling behind my eyes. I can't help but defy Mona's orders.

"Oh, for Christsake," he mutters. He can't stand it when the tears flow; he thinks it's nothing but a manipulative ploy. "Stop the little girl act."

I want to kill him. I want to fucking kill him.

"You're the one who told me to get out," he continues, with maybe just a little heat behind his words. "You're the one who wants me to leave. I'm only doing what you want."

I explode. "I don't want you to *leave*! I want you to stop drinking! I want you to stop gambling! I want you to be a normal fucking person!"

He has the nerve to "*shhh*" me.

I give him one last chance to explain last week's discovery. My voice lowers, but wavers with rage. Through clenched teeth, I growl, "And I want to know why a married man would need that book."

"*Fuckin' hell!*" he screams. "Here." He slams the check in front of me and then the door behind him.

Holding my head in both hands, I sob to the point of exhaustion. It takes forever before I de-escalate to a mere simmer, my mind a flatline, unable to process the deluge of thoughts and emotions assaulting my brain.

The newspaper I've been weeping over is open to the Religion section. Through the tears I notice several ads for alternative-type churches like Unity and Religious Science. There seems to be quite a metaphysical community here. The old guy's church I've been going to is okay, but I need one with better connections, a more direct line to God. Though my divine guidance so far has pretty much sucked.

I'll try someplace new tomorrow. Tomorrow will be better. The hospice assigned me a home care patient to visit in the afternoon, so that's something to look forward to. But first I have to get through the rest of this fucking day.

7.

A church in a middle school? This is the address from the newspaper; it must be the right place. After deliberating in the car for a few minutes, I figure what the hell and decide to follow some signs that lead to a room across from the cafeteria.

Uh-oh. Two church ladies jump on me before my second foot crosses the threshold. The chipper one in the wild blue and green print muumuu is the official greeter.

"Welcome! I'm Reverend Sandy. This is Reverend Judy."

I nod and glance around, casing the joint. Shit. There aren't enough people here to be anonymous.

"And your name is?" Reverend Judy wants to know.

I'd love to say Margaret Fleming, the fake name I give to men I don't feel like talking to in bars. Is it wrong to give a fake name in church?

I deem it is, and reluctantly admit, "Linda."

She smiles at the new meat and hands me a couple of papers. "Here's some information about our church...."

"Okay."

"We're having a pot luck dinner next Thursday night at Reverend Sandy's house. You're welcome to join us. The directions are on the flyer."

Pot luck? Unless by "pot," she means marijuana, I don't think I can make it.

Reverend Judy excuses herself and heads to the front of the room, leaving Reverend Sandy to handle the interrogation: How did you hear about our church? Do you live right here in Henderson? Where are you from?

I offer one- and two-word answers as I fretfully watch the people who were once milling around now settling in. At this point, all the aisle seats are taken and God forbid I have to sit next to someone.

"I'd better grab a seat," I tell her, as if I can't wait for the action to begin.

The folding chairs are positioned way too close to each other, especially for a room this size. The only spot I can enjoy my one-arm's length comfort zone is right up there in the front row, so I grudgingly plant myself one chair over from a pretty, but severe-looking woman with blue eyes and a long, jet-black mane. In my opinion, a lighter color would be more flattering, softer on the face. Thank God my mother's not here. *She needs to cut that goddamn hair*, I can hear her say, in the booming voice she uses to address her boyfriend. He may be half deaf, but the rest of the world isn't, I'm always reminding her. Boyfriend. The guy's pushing seventy, has a pig valve in his heart; I think the word "boyfriend" is about fifty years too late. I peruse my reading material, happy for a reason to avoid eye contact, but not at all happy about being front and center.

Reverend Judy takes her place at the podium. "Good morning, everyone!"

People reply "Good morning, Reverend Judy" in unison, like we're about to start an AA meeting.

"Before we begin, I'd like you to welcome our guest today." I'm hoping she's referring to someone else, but she looks straight at me. "Would you introduce yourself?" she asks in a softer voice, because after all, I'm like two feet away from her.

Hell, no! But I take a breath and open my mouth.

"Go ahead—stand up, please."

It's an effort to keep my eyeballs from rolling clear back to my brain stem. I rise and turn to see thirty mugs smiling at me like they can't wait to be my new best friend. I'd feel better if they'd all give me the finger. I grant them a quick, "Hi, I'm Linda," and plunk myself back down.

Reverend Judy reminds us about Thursday night's dinner and announces some other events of interest, but I can't pay attention because my church phobia is kicking in big-time and it's not even like I'm surrounded with pictures of Jesus or anything. I have to get out of here.

Soon the lights go off and we're told to close our eyes and relax for a few minutes in silent meditation. New Age music fills the room, a tad louder than warranted. After two deep, cleansing breaths, I peek over at Morticia Addams next to me. Her eyes are closed.

Wait a minute... I turn to spy on the rest of the congregation. Everyone's eyes are closed—Reverend Judy's, Reverend Sandy's, everyone's! Can I pull this off?

Yes, I can do this. With a pounding heart, I steal my own pocketbook off the floor, and like Tippi Hedren in an attic full of sparrows, I ever-so-cautiously tiptoe toward the door. Once out in the freedom of the sunshine, I pick up the pace until I'm practically sprinting to the car, then tear off as if I'd shot a liquor store clerk.

At the first red light, I crack myself up thinking how someday I'll tell little Connor the story of his granny's daring escape from a roomful of meditating parishioners. I'll end the tale with, "And when they opened their eyes—*poof!*—the new girl was gone!"

§ § §

I could go home, or if I hurry, I can still make the service at the old guy's church. I definitely need a spiritual boost today, so I shoot from Green Valley up to East Sahara, and make it there in no time. Not much traffic on a Sunday morning—all the fun people are still asleep. While I drive, I rack my brain trying to think of any other life event that warranted the act of tiptoeing, and come up with nothing.

The usher opens the front door and hands me this morning's program. Even though I've been coming here almost every Sunday for the past several months, I am thankful that my exchange with him involves nothing more than a nod.

Good—my favorite seat in the back of the sanctuary is free. Of course, it's on the aisle, so I can sneak out before the end when they all hold hands and sing. There's a cute little baby in the row in front of me, held by a woman I imagine to be her grandmother. Now, *she* looks like a grandmother—not hip and sexy-looking like me.

The baby's wearing a cute little dress, which should be enough, but the headband with a flower in the front, the pierced earrings, and the bracelet are overkill, if you ask me. A bracelet on an infant? I know I'm totally into self-adornment, but I need the ornamentation. Funky earrings divert attention from my crappy hair. If I'm wearing a beautiful necklace, no one will notice my double chin. Toe rings on my second and third digits detract from my oversized big toes.

But earrings and a bracelet on a baby who can hardly hold her head up? Yikes—if being three months old in itself doesn't make you cute enough, will this poor kid ever be able to please her parents? Where is her mother, anyway? Schlepping her four-year-old sister to one of those creepy Jon-Benet beauty pageants, no doubt. I know who I'm praying for today.

The old guy welcomes us, and I realize I like him because he never seems to be in a particularly cheery mood; it's almost like we've displeased him in some way. Reverend Judy and Reverend Sandy should take a lesson—make us work for your good graces. Maybe the thrill really is in the chase.

The topic for this Sunday's sermon is "Finding Love in a Neurotic World." Perfect. Our grumpy leader directs us through today's affirmations.

I avoid escapists—anyone addicted to alcohol, drugs, excessive gambling, or sexual players. Well, this message is about three years too late.

I avoid anyone who is in a constant state of denial. He doesn't have a problem. What makes you think he has a problem?

I avoid anyone who constantly uses profanity.

That's it—game over. Once again, I lift my pocketbook from the floor, and this time my departure is less covert. Church is just not working out for me.

8.

My new hospice patient lives in one of those developments for people age fifty-five plus. I drive slowly past a collection of tightly packed one-story structures with meticulously groomed cactus gardens in search of number 1385. There it is. An amusing lawn ornament sticks up from the pebbles, strategically placed near the sidewalk to ensure it captures the attention of passers-by. It's a wooden image of a squatting Dalmatian, with bold letters warning, "Not here!"

All I know about this woman is her name is Lola, she's eighty-three, she has some kind of pulmonary problem, and I like her already—nothing sets me off like dog shit on my shoe. Why do people think it's okay for their animals to crap wherever they want? That was my pet peeve when I had a lawn back in Albany. And though I grew up with a dog in the house, a pet peeve is the only pet I'll ever have in adult life. The licking, the sniffing—no thank you. Some people think I'm positively immoral for not embracing the animal kingdom; I like to think I'm a lovely person.

I've been so self-absorbed lately, I look forward to focusing on someone else for a change. The greatest gift you can give anyone is your full attention, I've learned. People in general are starved for it, especially old people. This will be good for me.

I ring the doorbell, figuring it'll take her a while to answer. The door opens presently by a tall and slender, but not frail-looking woman with cornflower eyes and thick, light brown hair that apparently will never turn more than half gray. Thin plastic tubing wraps around her ears and up into her nose.

"Hi, Lola? I'm Linda."

Her welcoming expression is one I normally associate with trespassing Jehovah's Witnesses.

"I'm from the hospice." *Hospice*, I said, not the goddamn IRS.

"They told me you'd be coming," she mutters, turning back into the house. The door remains open, so I follow her, closing it behind me. The hum of her oxygen machine merges with the din of the air conditioner, which she has cranked. Although it's still quite hot this time of year, she's wearing a sweater, slacks, and socks. In my sundress, I feel overexposed.

Lola points to a sandy-colored couch with a delicate turquoise and maize pattern, her way of saying, "Make yourself comfortable." She sits on the matching love seat.

I look around, taking in the Southwest décor—certainly not your typical old-lady funeral parlor furniture. But unlike many elderly people back east, Lola hasn't lived in the same house for the past several decades. Five years ago, I bet this whole area was nothing but dirt, dust, and rocks.

"You have a beautiful home," I comment with sincerity.

"Thank you. It will do."

"My mother would love a house like this."

"There are plenty for sale in the neighborhood. She can buy one, if she can afford it."

I don't think she can, but I keep the thought to myself. We sit in silence while Lola eyeballs me. I'm okay with that. I realize that the patients themselves are not necessarily the ones who've requested a volunteer; often it's the family, and I can't blame her for being skeptical or suspicious. Granny hated having strangers in her house, and she made no effort to hide her irritation when nurses from the hospice stopped in, especially if they dared to show up during her soaps. She'd downright ignore them until the commercials, when they had exactly two and a half minutes to check her vitals or whatever the hell they came to bother her for.

"The colors in here work well together," I comment. "I like your taste."

She frowns. "This is my daughter's doing. They sold all my furniture before they moved me here."

"Where did you come from?"

"Seattle."

"I've been there!" I exclaim, happy to have stumbled on some common ground. "I have a fridge magnet of the Space Needle."

Lola doesn't care, but I do. Seattle was the first trip Bastard Husband and I took together, six weeks after we met. From there we rode the ferry up to Victoria, Canada, a country he felt a special bond with because "New Zealand is Australia's Canada." To proclaim his support for the underdog, he bought a T-shirt that had "*Eh?*" in giant red letters across the chest, a maple leaf in the middle, and "It's better than saying, '*Huh?*'" at the bottom. Like an enthusiastic fan at a rock concert, he changed into it immediately, and I took his picture at the parliament house with a young woman dressed as Queen Victoria. We were so in love.

"I bet you don't miss all that rain," I say. "You must like waking up to sunshine every morning."

"No. I don't like the sun."

Lola has the face of a statue that's grown tired of standing around. I may be a regular Dale Carnegie with store clerks and service personnel, but I can't seem to break the ice with her.

This one's a long shot. "Do you follow any of the soap operas?"

She glares at me as if I asked whether she's into watching kiddie porn.

Wasn't this supposed to be a better day? Let's see, so far I've had two failed church experiences and now a hospice patient who doesn't like my stinkin' looks. I sigh.

"That's a pretty dress," Lola comments.

Her compliment jars me. "Thanks. It used to be one of my favorites, but I hardly ever wear it now." Nervous energy propels me to elaborate. "I once walked out of the ladies' room at work with the back of this dress accidentally tucked up in my underwear. One of my coworkers caught me halfway down the hall. It was pretty embarrassing."

What are these stupid words coming out of my mouth? Should I tell her about the time my sister pointed out my giant wedgie in the shopping mall? I thought it was my thong that I felt, but no, I had half my skirt crammed up my ass. Yeah, maybe she'd enjoy hearing that story, too. I'm an idiot.

Lola stares at me with the wonder of a young child scrutinizing an amputee; not only can she tell something's horribly wrong, she didn't know people like that even existed. Then unpredictably, she softens. "I bet you have a nice husband at home," she says.

Where the hell did that come from? I look at her blankly, and then as if on cue, shatter into a million tears—wailing, heaving, bawling uncontrollably. I have no idea what her reaction is because I've buried my face in my lap and it's staying there forever.

I can't stop crying. Every time I almost gain a sense of composure, I start in again. I'm supposed to be cheering her up—this woman who may not live until Thanksgiving—and here I am blubbering like they've cancelled *Guiding Light*. *"How'd it go with your volunteer, Lola?" "Well, quite frankly, she's a fucking mess. Next time, how 'bout sending someone without the mental problems?"*

What am I going to do? God forgive me, but when I finally look up, could you please make her be dead? I'll call the hospice and everyone will assume I've been crying because of poor Lola's passing. Or, please God, you can even take me—what do I have to live for? Just get me out of this.

"I'm sorry, I'm sorry," I sob, and after what seems to be about an hour and a half, I courageously lift my head to find her…grinning broadly like this is most fun she's had in ages. There's compassion in her eyes, so I can tell she's not being mean or anything. But what the hell?

"There's Kleenex if you need it," she says, motioning to the box on the coffee table in front of me. She must have placed it there when I was lost in the flood.

"Thank you." I try to control my breathing, but an errant quiver escapes intermittently.

"Will you sit with me on the patio while I smoke?" she asks, as if the experience has been so damn enjoyable she needs a cigarette afterward. "You can tell me all about it."

We both rise. Lola pulls the tubes from her nostrils and turns off the oxygen machine; I tug on my dress to make sure it hasn't hiked up into a body cavity. I follow her out to the patio, where we sit at a glass topped table looking out to a hill that appears to have the consistency of kitty litter.

That reminds me! "I love your little sign out front," I say, still sniffing.

She smirks. "I do, too. I saw that in a catalog and I had to have it."

Now there's the ice breaker I should have gone for: *You hate dog shit? So do I!*

Lola lights a Virginia Slims and I put up the invisible golden shield of protection I read about in my spiritual books to safeguard

me from the secondhand smoke. I imagine a chest x-ray would re-
veal an assortment of ironic black spots on my lungs, a mordant
testimony to my altruistic hospice work. Someday, no doubt, I'll find
myself lying in the inpatient unit, breathing through a hole in my
throat while some Chatty Cathy volunteer hovers over me yakking
away about nothing. I won't be able to tell her to shut up because, of
course, they'll have removed my voicebox—my karmic payback for
years of spouting profanities. Yeah, that's a loving God.

"So you don't have a nice husband at home," Lola says. "Do you
have a mean husband at home?"

I can tell she wants the dirt, so I decide to lay it all out there—
once you've had a meltdown on a stranger's couch, what do you
have to lose?   I tell her how we met in Buffalo and the cosmic Michael McNeil story in Niagara Falls that I thought was surely the
universe's way of telling us we were destined to be together. I go on
about living in Laramie and Utah, the good and the bad—the hikes,
road trips, and yoga, as well as the name calling, water throwing,
and other crazed behavior.

She's all ears, and I'm not surprised that she's so enthralled with
the details of my life. Every old lady I've known has enjoyed hearing
about my pathetic relationships, and they took even more satisfaction in providing counsel. "A man with a ponytail? You don't want
to go out with someone like that," advised Chickie, my first hospice
patient. She didn't care that he looked like Johnny Depp. And once
I learned he was banned from Price Chopper for catching a buzz off
the gas in the Redi-Whip, he kind of lost his appeal with me, too. I
know how to pick 'em.

Lola takes it all in, sparing me the commentary. Now and then
she interjects a question, not with the obviously probing tone of a
therapist, or Mona's crusty, "Why did you marry him in the first
place?" but with the disinterest of a sleuth.

She recaps to ensure understanding. "So you both moved to Las Vegas, then he went to New Zealand for the summer, and then he came back. Is that right?"

"Yes."

"And Monday morning you told him to get out and stay out."

"Right."

"You've been through a lot with him."

I nod. She gets it.

Lola sits back in her chair and deliberates. "So what happened that made you decide enough is enough?"

Shit. I don't want to start crying again, but it's clear she's expecting a response. Though I've analyzed it a million times in my head, I have yet to make a verbal disclosure. I take a deep breath and vow to answer her question with not as much as a whimper.

"I found something," I start to explain. "Last Sunday night I stayed up to watch TV after he went to bed. I noticed his backpack on the floor in the hall and, I don't know why, I felt the urge to look in it.

"I'm not that kind of person," I assure her, lest she think I'll soon be rummaging through her underwear drawer, "but for some reason, I was drawn to it."

Without breaking eye contact Lola reaches for her lighter and fires up yet another one.

"So I opened it and right there, right on top, was a book…called *The Guide to Picking Up Girls*. I don't get it. It's not like he's a flirt or anything. He's certainly not a ladies' man. I don't think he particularly likes women to begin with. So why would he need *The Guide to Picking Up Girls*? That's what I want to know.

"I'll tell you, he will never find anyone as good as me. Never! Who else would put up with his crap? And I've put up with a lot. But that's one thing I will not tolerate." I'm not done.

"I could kill him! I could…" oooh, I want to swear so bad, "just *kill* him!"

I've worked myself into a rage. Lola coolly gazes out the window and then at me.

"Let me think about this," she states, with the assurance of a business consultant who needs to consider all the angles before proposing a plan of action. "Are you coming back next Sunday?"

"If you want me to."

"Of course, I do."

At first I think she must be kidding; I can't imagine why she'd care to see me ever again. But then I think of Little Betsy's hemorrhoids on my birthday, and it all makes sense: One woman's bastard husband is another woman's distraction from chronic pulmonary disease. There really is a divine order to the universe, everything really is exactly as it's supposed to be.

"Okay, Lola. I'll see you next week."

She smiles. I guess my visit did cheer her up. Maybe I'm not such a bad volunteer after all.

9.

Mona's been fragile lately. This divorce shit is getting to her.

"Thank you for helping me," she says, sitting at the table in my apartment. "I started my resume, but…" She shakes her head and pushes some papers toward me. "It's *drek*."

"No problem," I tell her. "I can write these things in my sleep."

I can. Before GE I worked for an international corporate outplacement firm. I led two- and three-day workshops on job search techniques for "displaced workers" and "employees in transition," unwilling participants in their company's latest "downsizing" efforts. Talk about euphemisms.

During the course of the training, I helped everyone from executives to sweatshop personnel put their resumes together. My background in technical writing came in handy; I could produce a work of resume art from nothing but a verbal mind dump. Not that I exaggerated or anything, I just seem to have a natural talent for making people look the best they possibly can, on paper anyway.

I actually liked that type of work. People came to the workshops full of anxiety and left feeling confident, having gained solid interviewing skills and with a well-crafted resume in hand. It was gratifying to see the transformation. Of course, the idea of my teaching job search skills was kind of ironic, considering a job is the last thing

126

I'd ever want in life. Half the time I could hardly hide my jealousy. *You mean they're giving you twenty-six weeks' severance pay and you get to collect unemployment?* I swear there's an imposter princess in a faraway kingdom wearing my tiara. When I find her, I'm going to kick her ass.

"So," I say, scanning Mona's notes, "you're a substitute teacher in the Clark County School District. Tell me about that."

She frowns. "They call me and I go in. What else can I say? How can you fill a whole page with that?"

"Relax. I've done resumes for factory workers in Vermont who for thirty years literally did nothing but cut the cheese."

Mona ekes out a smile and starts fanning herself with a manila folder. "You're funny."

I continue my interrogation and discover that besides having spitballs shot at her for seventeen years, she briefly sold jewelry in her friend's shop.

"I can definitely see you in sales," I tell her. "You're the most aggressive person I know." I consider my statement and add, "I mean that in a good way." It's true, though. No one can talk a waitress into accepting an expired twenty percent off coupon like Mona. I wish I had balls like that.

"I did all right," she admits. "I made a sale almost every time."

"Hmm…" I play with the words I've jotted down. "Would you say you 'achieved a successful closing ratio of approximately 90 percent'?" This is fun for me—first a little detective work, then we put the pieces of the puzzle together.

"I also worked on fundraisers for my breast cancer survivors' group, but all I did was hand out brochures and talk to people."

"Don't minimize yourself," I scold. "I'd say you…'solicited funds to raise awareness of breast cancer prevention and treatment.'"

She nods, acknowledging she's onto the game we're playing.

"So what type of job are you looking for?" I ask.

My little exercise is starting to exhaust her. "I don't know. I'll work for anyone who will take me."

I put down my pen. "No, Mona. Think about what you *want* to do. What do you want to be when you grow up?"

Mona doesn't want to play anymore. "I'm fifty-five years old! I thought I *was* grown up!" She releases an exasperated sigh. "I don't want to do this. I don't want to have to look for a job. I want my old life back!"

So many tears have been shed at this table. For once, they're not mine.

"It's okay." I reach for the Kleenex. "Here. Give me a couple of minutes to put something together."

I scribble away. Mona sniffs.

I understand her bewilderment. Several women in our divorce group are in their fifties and sixties; some have been homemakers their whole adult lives. Now a stone's throw from retirement age, they're thrust into the job market kicking and screaming, their arsenal of experience consisting of titles such as room mother and PTA committee chair.

Mona's ahead of the game. She has a bachelor's degree and a career to speak of, though subbing for seventeen years would hardly place her on the fast track. Subbing won't cut it now, though. I'm sure it doesn't pay much, and once her divorce becomes final, Mona will need benefits. Because of her history of breast cancer, she'll pay a fortune if she has to insure herself.

I'm way ahead of the game. I'm only forty-six, I'm well educated, and even I have to admit I have an impressive work history. Too bad about the lousy attitude.

"Okay," I say. "Your resume should start with an overview, a brief encapsulation of what you're all about. Tell me how this sounds.

Over 15 years of diverse experience encompassing teaching, sales, fundraising, and event planning. Extensive local networking contacts and an intimate knowledge of community resources. Possess a friendly, outgoing personality suitable for public relations." I look up from the paper. "It's not quite there yet, but it's a start. Is that you?"

"That's the best version of me I've ever heard," she says. The clouds have parted.

"My bullshitting skills are quite impressive," I state. "I should add them to my resume, don't you think?" Sometimes I amaze myself with the crap that comes out of my brain. And my mouth.

Just for fun, someday I'll write up my "authentic" resume—the version that reflects the real me. I'm sure prospective employers would be impressed by my Guiding Light Fan Club membership, not to mention my second place finish last year in a pretty feet contest in New Orleans. And a mammogram technician once told me she's never squished anyone's breasts as flat as mine without peeling the person off the ceiling.

Those extraordinary qualifications would probably get more attention than my current resume, which nobody here seems bright enough to understand. Last Monday I had an interview with a screener from the human resources department at Stations Casinos. We're talking about a training job and she has no idea what a goddamn instructional designer does. No surprise—she's like twenty-four-years old, probably making about eight dollars an hour. All she wants to know is whether I've ever worked in a casino before.

It's clear these casino people would rather promote a keno runner than hire someone who actually has a professional training background. Why do they think their industry is so goddamn special, beyond the comprehension of anyone from the outside world? I worked in the GE corporate headquarters, for Christsake. Did I know anything about Six Sigma process improvement before I started working there? I have a feeling I can wrap my head around a few slot machines.

"I'll type everything up and email you this tomorrow."

Mona appreciates my efforts, but has had enough of the spotlight. "So how about you? What's going on with you?"

Shit. I liked it better when she was the center of attention. "I got an offer yesterday…"

Her eyebrows arch.

I'll just blurt it out. "Selling pre-arranged funerals. You know, caskets…and, um…graves." Though the idea's been living in my head for a few days, it does sound a little whacko now that I'm saying it out loud.

"You're not going to take it." Mona shakes her head and then gives me a side glance. "Are you?"

"Um, well, I kind of already told them I would. I have to go in to fill out the paperwork Saturday morning."

She rolls her eyes. Parental disappointment. That's what I want from my only friend. "Linda, really. Working for a *cemetery*?"

"It's a 'memorial park.'" I can't keep a straight face.

Mona hardly knows me and already she can tell I may be a brilliant navigator of someone else's life, but I have absolutely no sense of judgment when it comes to my own.

"I'd be helping people," I say, building a weak defense. "It's a logical next step from being a hospice volunteer."

"Do you think this is really the best use of your talents?"

"No, *Mom*!" Now I'm ready to cry. "I *don't* think it's the best use of my talents, but no one here seems to recognize what my talents are."

Actress, ballerina, figure skater…no, I'm pretty sure cemetery plot saleswoman was not on the list of what I wanted to be when I grew up.

"Have you ever thought of subbing?" Mona asks. "They're desperately looking for teachers. You'll be able to work every day. I do."

Suddenly selling graves seems downright appealing.

"Me?" Substitute teacher was not on that list, either. I have to steer her away from this crazy idea. "Don't you need some kind of certification?"

"No, just a bachelor's degree. In anything. Or sixty-three credits toward an education degree."

Oh, please. "Aren't there kids involved?"

"No, Linda. Why would there be children in schools?"

Nice. My endearing sarcasm has worn off on her.

"I don't think so," I say. I like kids that are cute and well-behaved, but I bet she has to teach the bratty ones, too. I explore the horrifying possibilities. "What if they pee their pants? What if they throw up at their desk? Oh, my God—*what if they have lice???*"

"So teach middle school or high school. They're usually toilet trained by that age."

"I don't know. Don't think I'm evil or anything. I mean, I *love* babies. And old people. I like people when they're coming and going. Everyone in between gets on my nerves."

She's back to the eyes rolling.

"Not you," I add. "But go figure—the infants and the old folks are the very ones spitting up and pissing their pants all the time." I give her a moment to reflect on my uncanny percipience. "I'm not like your nice Jewish friends, am I?"

She slowly shakes her head. "You should sign up at that comedy club you go to."

"I'm not trying to be funny, Mona." I like her; she puts up with me. "Okay, I'll think about subbing. What does it pay?" I can't believe I'm asking.

"Ninety dollars a day."

Ninety dollars a day. That's one-fifth of my last per diem rate back East, and I never had to wipe up puke for that gig.

"You could do it for a while anyway," Mona reasons.

"You mean while I look for a real job?" I realize my question insinuates she hasn't worked a real job in seventeen years. "I'm, sorry," I say. "I want my old life back, too."

§ § §

Jim, the man who hired me to be his grave peddler, seems nice enough. He's not nearly as sickening as the guy who interviewed me to sell timeshares, but he still has that icky salesman aura about him.

"Linda, I'm absolutely tickled to have you aboard," he says, handing me a thick stack of papers.

Tickled? Who are you—Paul Lynde?

I force an anemic smile and recall Groucho Marx's tenet. Anybody who wants me that bad—be it a prospective employer or an aspiring lover—surely is no one I want any part of.

I spend about an hour filling out tax forms, reviewing policies and procedures, signing this and that, and avoiding eye contact with the urns and markers that decorate the sales office.

"You can start on Tuesday, right? That's just super," Jim says, checking his watch. "Ooh…I'd better scoot. Gotta catch a two-fifteen flight. I'll be back Monday night, though, so Tuesday morning we'll dig right in."

I'd be semi-amused if that was supposed to be a joke. I have to get out of this.

"Here," he continues, with a wide grin that induces me to suppress a wince. "The bible. Required reading for all the new team members."

Team members? He can't mean me. I'm not what you'd call a

team player. Compromising sucks, and when people don't see things my way, I secretly question their mental capacity. Sometimes not-so-secretly. Granted, I was on a team when I worked at GE, but that was different—those people were intelligent enough to appreciate my valuable insights.

I take my copy of *Close More Sales! Persuasion Skills That Boost Your Selling Power*. Required reading—kiss my ass. Nobody tells me what to read.

Once again I'm fighting back the tears. I toy with the idea of melting down like I did at Lola's house so maybe he'll think I'm too emotionally unstable for the job, but he's used to people blubbering away. All in a day's work for him. Shit.

"See you Tuesday," I say.

§§§

Four hours later I'm back at the "memorial park," sitting in my car outside the main building across from the mausoleum. I'm the only one around; since it's Saturday, the sales office closed at noon. It's three-thirty, and if Jim's flight was at two-fifteen, he's probably in the air by now. It should be safe to make the call.

"Hi, Jim. It's Linda. Gee…after we met this morning, another company offered me a position that I really need to take. But thank you…you know…It's just that I, um…this new opportunity, it's a better match for my background. So, well, thank you. Hope you're having a good flight. Bye!"

I'm almost free. One more dirty deed to go.

I creep up to the front door of the office, slip the "bible" under the welcome mat, and hightail it back to my car like a teenager who's abandoned a newborn on the church steps. I'm becoming quite the getaway driver; next I'll be robbing 7-Elevens. I may have to, if

I don't find a job soon. A real job.

This wasn't a real job. I did the right thing. Plus, how can I work for someone who says "tickled"?

10.

Lola called first thing this morning and said she's not feeling well enough for me to come over. She wasn't up for a visit last Sunday, either. She's probably afraid to let me in her house again—who could blame her? I imagine she called the hospice and said, "Please, no more of that one," and they don't have the heart to tell me.

Maybe it's just as well. I'm feeling down today and "at risk" for another crash. You can be forgiven the first time you splatter your emotions all over someone's living room, but do it twice and you're pretty much a nutcase who needs to get some help.

I called him last night. That was a mistake. His stupid *Economists* are still coming and I found a few more of his things. I'm going up to Utah next week to see my girlfriends—I told him I can drop this stuff off, if he wants.

"Okay," he replied. "I'll leave my car unlocked. You know where I park in the faculty lot. You can drop it off there." Conversation over.

I hung up deflated, but really, what did I think he would say? *Oh, Linda, my darling, I fear I've made a dreadful mistake. Please forgive me. Find it in your heart to take me back.* Yes, as a matter of fact, that would have been nice to hear.

That bastard. How can he just roll along and act like…oh, well? I know how. I've done it myself.

A few years ago, I went out with this guy named Mike, a free-spirited Deadhead who was what my sister Lori and I would call "a good soul," a term more insulting than endearing. A good soul is someone who means well, but will never quite make the cut, no matter how hard he tries.

Mike was a lot younger than me—at the time, I had two kids and a boyfriend all in their twenties. I met him at a bar in Connecticut while I worked at GE, and saw him during the week while I was down there. After spending all day with process engineers, I found his tie-dyed approach to life refreshing. While I went through the motions of building some kind of career, by age twenty-eight he'd already met his life-long goal of working as a ramp agent for Southwest Airlines, a position I helped him secure with my expert resume writing skills. I've written resumes for a lot of boyfriends.

We traveled some—to Denver, Phoenix, San Francisco—and for the most part had a pretty good time. But we were together far longer than we should have been, and after the first year, my interest in him developed a slow leak. Eventually he drove me nuts. Nuances I once found mildly amusing became barely tolerable, until they finally annoyed the hell out of me.

How does that happen? The same person I admired for his laid-back temperament now lacked ambition. He sniffed too often. He walked like a duck. He breathed too loud.

Because Mike was a good soul, I didn't want to hurt his feelings, so it took me forever to finally break it off with him. Once I did, I never looked back; the relationship had long passed its expiration date and freedom was a relief. I breezily skipped away and never gave him another thought.

A couple of months later he tracked me down in my hotel room outside of Buffalo; Courtney had given him my number. Unfortunate timing—I'd met Bastard Husband about two weeks before and was positively giddy from having found the love of my life. Mike and I chatted politely and I wished him well, while my new beau kissed the back of my neck in anticipation of another romp in the sack.

Poor Mike. We've all made that call. Our hearts pound as we press the buttons on the phone, perhaps we cower and hang up once or twice before it rings. We know full well the effort is in vain, our desired outcome never will be fulfilled, yet we endure the tortures of this pitiful exercise in self-abuse. It rewards us with fresh drama to re-enact and analyze over and over in our minds, and muffles the voice of reason that says, *Turn the fucking page.*

I feel like I'm Mike Peterson now, like the karma bank finally caught up with me and has made an automatic withdrawal. But I was never in love with Mike, I knew from the beginning we were merely marking time together. I never suggested we get married or promised to spend the rest of my life with him or told him that the force of the universe is what brought us together.

I'm not Mike Peterson. I shouldn't have to turn the fucking page.

§ § §

I checked out yet another church today, this one run by a bunch of female psychics. I liked it. They all took turns speaking about spiritual topics like abundance and gratitude and intuition. Occasionally my thoughts wandered and I realized you probably shouldn't think, "That woman should soften her hair color" when the focus of your attention can read your mind.

People were nice enough, meaning they left me alone, and I got a kick out of the recorded music they selected to play. You know, after you've been thinking about God for a while, you hear "Love Me Tender" in a whole new way. Vegas is so cool. We pray sitting on folding chairs in strip malls, listening to Elvis—no wooden pews or scary organ music in clammy old cathedrals for us. And when they started a John Edwards *Crossing Over* communicate-with-the-dead kind of thing, I thought, can this place get any better?

"The lady in the green top, may I come to you?" asked the clairvoyant who held the floor at the moment.

Thrilled to have been chosen, I sat bolt upright and answered, "Yes!"

"There's an older woman around you, a grandmother figure, I believe."

I nodded, a bit freaked out, but in a good way. After Lola called this morning, I swear I felt a spirit around me, and had a feeling it might be Granny.

"She says you've been focusing on someone else. Does that make sense to you?"

I nodded again.

"She says to tell you that your needs are important, too. It's time to do something for yourself." The woman looked off beyond the last row of seats, then back at me. "I hope that message is helpful."

That *was* Granny in my apartment this morning! I knew it.

My exuberance faded when the sermon ended with the dreaded finale of holding hands and singing that stupid "Let There Be Peace on Earth" song. Even if it were socially acceptable to don a pair of latex gloves before clutching the hands of complete strangers, I'd still think that's the dorkiest thing you could possibly do.

Afterward I headed over to the hospice, as I do every Sunday afternoon, except for the day I visited Lola. I'm glad I have somewhere to go. Saturdays and Sundays can be depressing for divorced people. I remember not knowing what to do with myself on weekends after Chris and I split up. There was no one to play with—the kids were off with their friends, and my friends were busy with family activities or home improvement projects. Back then I worked Monday through Friday and at least had laundry and household chores to catch up on. But now I wonder, would it kill them to run Oprah and the soaps seven days a week?

The hospice was quiet today; usually it's filled with visitors on Sunday afternoons. I started off as always by making the rounds with the water cart. Though it's rare that a patient actually wants or needs fresh ice water, the task gives me an excuse to see who's still there, who's awake, who has family members in need of some light conversation. Every room in the facility has a bed for the patient and a day bed for anyone who wants to spend the night, so I was thrown when I saw two hospital beds in one room, pushed right together. An elderly man occupied one, his wife the other. Evidently some people take that "till death do we part" vow to a level of synchronicity most of us have never considered.

Although they seemed to be having a grand time watching TV, lounging in their pajamas and sipping apple juice through a bendable straw, the scene depressed me as I imagined their poor kids, "kids" no doubt in their fifties or sixties, having to contend with both parents on their way out at the same time.

Later I stopped in to see Joan, a good-natured woman with whom I've had several pleasant exchanges. Joan graciously thanks me to no end whenever I bring her some sherbet from the kitchen, which I'm more than happy to do. Her two daughters were there with her today, packing up her belongings. They're all leaving tomorrow; Joan's going back to Maryland so the girls can take care of her in her remaining time. I was sorry to say good-bye, and even sadder knowing that only three months ago Joan was walking around minding her own business like a perfectly normal person. A diagnosis of pancreatic cancer changes everything in a flash.

So I've been in and out of a funk all day—what else is new? I have to go out tonight; I need an attitude adjustment. I think I'll go to Boomers, the bar on the west side of town that has open mic comedy on Sunday nights. Yeah, that seems like a good idea.

§ § §

Like all female bartenders in Las Vegas, the woman pouring my beer is a pretty young thing with enormous breasts that greet you long before her thousand-watt smile.

"How you doin' tonight?" she asks, with a sincerity that defies the haughtiness one might expect from someone that good-looking. I find Vegas refreshingly unpretentious, with a collective mood of acceptance. Beautiful people are everywhere—big deal—we're all here to have fun. I never feel unattractive or old. I suppose that's easy to say when your primary hangout is a hospice.

I head for the back room and take a seat against the far wall. The decor reminds me of an extremely low budget training room, with cheap folding tables and garage-sale dining room chairs facing a stage that's a one-step climb from floor level. Maybe thirty or forty people fill the room, many of whom are comics I recognize from previous visits. One or two give me a polite nod of recognition. I put on my "I'm with the band" air of confidence, even though there is no band. I'm with the DJ? Doesn't quite work.

The lights dim and the DJ plays a few seconds of an upbeat guitar riff. Marcus, the emcee, takes the stage. He's a good looking guy in his early thirties who's mentioned that by day he plays King Arthur in a show at the Excalibur. Marcus welcomes us and does his schtick to warm up the crowd for a few minutes, then shouts into the microphone, "Are you ready for your first comic tonight?" The crowd whoops in response.

One by one each comic takes the stage. The quality of the performances varies. A college kid destined to be a future yuppie tells a way-too-long and not very funny story about a recent problem with constipation. Cheap humor. Another guy named Shuli, who is somehow connected with the Howard Stern show, does a hilarious bit about his insecurities as a "five-foot-seven balding Jew" having sex with a domineering black woman. Some of the guys bomb, a few are seasoned comics getting in some stage time to hone their act or try out new material. Anything goes. It's all good.

"Anyone can perform here at Boomer's open mic night," Marcus explains at some point during each show. "Sign up tonight, show up next Sunday to confirm your spot, and the following week, you, too, can be doing stand-up comedy."

Sometimes during the summer I wondered if I could get up there and do that. I must have some kind of stage presence from all those years leading training workshops. And I seem to be able to make people laugh; Mona thinks I'm funny and my friends at GE thought I was a riot. Not that there was anything else to laugh at there.

A skinny guy whose shorts are falling halfway down his ass has some really funny material, but he breaks the momentum every time he stops his act to read from his notes. I'd probably be better than some of these people, but it's easy to criticize from the audience. I'm sure it's quite another thing to be up there in front of everyone.

Wait… Could I get up there? I think of how I sent Johnny Carson my jokes when I was a kid. Is this one of those goals I've subconsciously aspired to all these years, but never thought was possible?

Between comics Marcus entertains the crowd with material taken from today's headlines. Okay, I could never do topical humor. I don't know what the hell is going on—I can barely keep it together in my own little world. Sure, I subscribe to two newspapers, but mainly for the comics and the crosswords. CNN? I get my news from the E! channel. And the last thing I'd ever want to talk about is politics. One time some blowhard in the Irish pub at Green Valley

Ranch tried to rope me into a conversation about global affairs. To get him going, I said, "I like that Tony Blair, but don't you think he was a lot funnier in Monty Python?"

Hmmm... I should be able to come up with some kind of act. God knows between ex-husbands and ex-boyfriends alone there's enough material for an HBO special. Oh, but could I really do it?

Tonight's headliner, a comic named Joe Lowers, takes the stage. This guy is a professional; I've overheard him talking to Shuli about his gigs on the road. Joe's one of the older guys here—close to forty, I bet—and he seems really nice. He says hi when he sees me. Playing heavily off the audience, Joe appears to ad lib his entire act, with no fear of looking like an idiot as he dances and jumps around. I laugh heartily, sometimes at nothing but the mere sight of him. He's good.

After Joe's through with his crazy antics, Marcus returns to the stage one last time. "Thank you all for coming out tonight. Let's give a big hand to all our comics," he says, clapping enthusiastically. "Don't forget we're here at Boomers every Sunday. Comics, I'll be taking sign-ups for two weeks from tonight. See me if you're interested. Good night, everybody! See you next week!"

Go ahead, sign up, the voice inside me says. I can't tell if it's the voice of reason or the voice that's been sending my life to the shitter for the past few years. It's probably the latter, since the voice of reason seems to make only cameo appearances. But maybe this is exactly what I need. Granny's right—I should do something for myself. What a kick it would be to pull this off. And if not here at Boomers, then where? No one gets heckled. People can bomb and the audience claps no matter what. The vibe is supportive, not at all competitive.

Joan's trip to Maryland tomorrow comes to mind. Life is short. I should give this a try.

The lights come up and we all file into the bar area. I linger there a while, eyeing a group of comics sitting at a banquette across from the bar. I'm not brave enough to hang with them as they wait to get their names in with Marcus, so I go back into the showroom, where he and the DJ are packing up their sound equipment.

"Hey, thanks for coming out tonight," Marcus says as he winds the microphone cord around his elbow.

"I, um, I want to sign up."

"You want to do a set?" He seems genuinely pleased. "That's great! We need female comics."

"Well, I'm not really a comic. I mean, this will be my first time."

"Awesome!" he says. "I'll put you down for two weeks from tonight. We'll start you out with five minutes. Be sure to show up next Sunday to confirm your spot."

"Okay."

"What's you're name?" Marcus asks, offering his hand.

I extend mine. I'm too nervous to care about germs right now. "Linda," I blurt.

"Well, great, Linda. We'll see you next Sunday."

Holy shit. What have I done now?

11.

Reality is setting in. Soon I have to stand in front of a roomful of people and not only hold their attention, but make them laugh. *Out loud.* Not smile or chuckle under their breath; snickers and soft tee-hees won't cut it. No, I have to come up with something so hilarious they'll actually emit audible sounds. And I have to do this for five whole minutes. What have I gotten myself into?

It shouldn't be this hard. I come from one of those families where everyone's a comedian. "You're eight years old?" my father would ask my little friends. "I'm surprised at you. When I was your age, I was ten!" Each new playmate we brought to the house was sub-jected to Daddy's repertoire of one-liners, straight from Yogi Berra's B-list. "I know your mother," he'd tell them. "We went to different schools together."

Daddy was a funny man. Funny ha-ha and funny odd. When he called to inform his sister about a death in the family, he was both at the same time.

"Joyce," he began to break the news, "how many uncles do we have?"

"Why, we have one uncle," she answered, to which he bellowed, *"WRONG!"*

My father would do anything to score a laugh—walk into walls, summon a waitress by calling, "Nurse!"—whatever it took. Daddy was always on, always looking for the perfect opportunity to quip, "Other than that, Mrs. Kennedy, how'd you like Dallas?" On the other hand, our mother's brand of humor is purely unintentional. She'll bolt from the couch to answer a phone that's ringing on the television, then yell *Bastard!* into the inevitable dial tone before slamming the receiver. Make a grammatical slip and she'll scream, *"Jesus Christ, I didn't bring you kids up to talk like that! What do you think, we live in a goddamn ghetto?"* And nothing's more entertaining than her deadpan explanation of why O.J. is innocent.

As the product of those two nuts, my brother and sisters and I all have a decent sense of humor. We have to. When we're together, we fiercely compete for center stage, each of us rushing to the punch line before a perceptive sibling beats us to it, since along with the formidable gene pool, we also share the same train of thought. No topic is off limits, no matter how vile or politically incorrect. We fearlessly let it rip, howling over dark ironies that would induce winces from normal people. We're always laughing our heads off; my brother has the snappiest comebacks and my sister Lori is a riot. But now that I think of it, does anyone laugh at *me*? Whatever made me think I'm a funny person?

I bought Judy Carter's book, *The Comedy Bible*, to help me get my act together. Now there's a bible I can use. It says not to tell stories, and to get to the punch line in as few words as you can. From my initial scribbles, I can already see the value of having a technical writing background. In tech writing, as in comedy, every word counts. Whoever thought that documenting Six Sigma processes and gas turbine specifications could actually help you write comedy? Every experience really does fit into the next; no effort is ever wasted. Life unfolds exactly as it should. Even when things seem totally fucked up, there's a good reason behind it all—we're just not hip to the complex infrastructure of the universe. That's why you have to have faith and trust that everything is in divine order. That's what my spiritual bookcase says. If it's not true, I'll be pissed as hell.

§§§

This morning I went to the psychic ladies' church again and afterward had a nice visit with Lola. We sat on her patio while she dragged on one cigarette after another as if she'd face harsh penalties if she fell short on the day's quota. As I once again put up my imaginary golden shield of protection, a slogan for an anti-smoking campaign came to me. It's both simple and effective: "Hospice patients smoke."

We talked a little about her life back in Seattle—Lola worked as a medical receptionist—and I tried to ask her questions about her family, but it was clear she was more interested in what I had to say. "Tell me how you're doing, dear. Any word from the husband?" she asked. I don't know if it was a coincidence that she'd just taken popcorn out of the microwave or if she was expecting another show, but I got the feeling she was slightly disappointed that my mental state was, for the moment, stable.

The truth is, it's been great to have something else consume my thoughts. Ever since I signed up with Marcus last week, I've been racking my brains trying to recall every wisecrack, every witticism, anything I've ever said that someone thought was mildly amusing. No doubt my tired mind appreciates the break from the obsessive Bastard Husband ruminations. Right now that record is out of heavy rotation. I didn't mention to Lola that next Sunday I'll be trying my hand at stand-up comedy. After my performance in her living room last time, I doubt she'd believe it anyway.

Tonight I go back to Boomers to confirm my time for next week.

Right now I'm sitting in Starbucks sorting through the pages of raw material I've generated over the past week. Nothing looks funny to me. Maybe I have a couple of semi-humorous lines. Maybe. You wouldn't believe how long it takes to put together five minutes of material.

After my second caffe mocha, I decide I'm sick of looking at my feeble attempts at comedy and begin to eavesdrop on an exchange two tables over, where a young employee is conducting an interview with an attractive woman who appears to be in her early fifties. Mona's been talking about Starbucks. They offer benefits as long as you work twenty hours a week, an appealing lure for people who've been displaced from a job or a husband, people who never dreamed they'd be looking to a coffee shop as a source of sustenance.

"Um, what would you do if you were going to be late for work?" I overhear the fresh-faced barista supervisor ask in a voice of authority I sense she is using for the first time.

The scene disturbs me. The lady smiles and nods, trying to make the best of the situation, but I know damn well she wasn't punching a clock in her last job. Every once in a while I see these people, so obviously underemployed. Older gentlemen working as bank tellers, perhaps aged out of their corporate positions, making a fraction of their former take-home pay. In their fifties and sixties, they find themselves obeying work rules designed for the ethics of teenagers, imposed by entry-level managers they should be mentoring. They put up with it only because they have to.

I discreetly face my palm in the job candidate's direction and send her positive vibrations. It's a queer gesture, I admit, but sometimes I swear I can feel the energy shoot straight through the center of my hand. I do it for people in wheelchairs, drivers waiting for roadside assistance, hospice patients sleeping through their penultimate afternoon on earth. I send healing to those who seem a little weary and may need a boost, and sometimes I send good thoughts to strangers for no other reason than I like their looks. I hope it works. I'll never really know.

So maybe for this woman, getting a job at Starbucks will be one of those experiences that fits right into the next in the big scheme of her life. Maybe she'll serve a java chip cappuccino to a rich and handsome man who turns out to be the love of her life. I hope so. If this is what's best, then I hope Barista Boss Lady deems her worthy of doling out lattes.

Please God, don't let it get to that point for me. My savings isn't going to last that much longer. Something has to give. And soon. I sent out some more resumes this week, and even ventured onto the school district's website to look into subbing, just so I can tell Mona I'm following up on her suggestion. She'll ask, believe me. Let's hope it doesn't come to that.

I turn my palm and direct good energy toward myself. *Stay positive. You can't be funny if you're worrying about your survival.*

§ § §

I watch the comics perform with a totally different eye now.

What are they doing with that microphone stand? How does that thing work? Do you twist it in the middle and then pull the rod up and down? Exactly how does the microphone fit into the stand? Do you just shove it in there? I'm not good at doing anything; I have no eye-hand coordination. I can barely open a box of pasta or carton of ice cream without making a mess of it. I'll probably spend half my set trying to place the mic into position. And the cord—I'll trip over that, guaranteed.

A comic channeling Andrew Dice Clay currently has the spotlight. I've seen this guy before. I don't think he's particularly funny, but he has good stage presence. He sure knows how to work the mic. Look at that—when he needs his hands to make gestures, he just slips it in the stand. Then he takes it out again no problem. And he's sucking on a Budweiser in between it all. The guy's a genius!

"I'm half Italian and half Puerto Rican," he says, setting up his punch line. "I got a big dick, but it smells."

Jesus. I hardly consider myself a prude, but *yuk*! That doesn't seem funny to me. The audience thinks it's funny, though. Shit. If people are laughing at this kind of crap, I doubt they'll see any humor in the reflections of a middle-aged grandmother.

After the show I hang around the banquette out in the bar area with the comics waiting to sign up with Marcus and those, like me, who wait to confirm their time for next Sunday. I try to act cool among all these young guys, though I doubt I'm pulling it off.

Smelly Dick Boy and I accidentally make eye contact. "How you doin', baby?" he wants to know.

"I'm doin' fine," I answer.

"You gonna sign up, sweetheart?"

Baby? Sweetheart? This kid can't be a day older than my son, Christopher. *Young man, I could be your mother.* "I'm going up next week," I tell him. "It'll be my first time."

"Yo, guys—this one's gonna pop her comedy cherry next week!" he says in a voice way too loud for my current level of confidence. I expect them all to turn with an expression that says, this old broad doesn't look funny to me.

"Sweet!" one of them says, extending his hand.

"Yeah, we need some babes around here," says another one.

I smile and do my secret palm energy thing to thank them for being so nice. I no longer have to pretend I'm *with* the band. I'm *in* the band.

12.

This is good; I need to get away. I've been driving myself nuts getting ready for Sunday night—analyzing, restructuring, and punching up my material. (It's *five minutes*, for God's sake.) Plus I want to get rid of his stuff. My apartment is my sacred space and I don't need his crap stinking up the joint.

Our old house in Utah looks the same. I could have headed directly to the faculty parking lot, but it takes such minimal effort—in this case, a three-block detour—to perpetuate my exercise in self-torture. Scabs from emotional wounds beg to be picked, and I willingly oblige, if only to confirm I'll still bleed. Sure enough, the sight of someone else's red Neon sitting in the driveway that used to be ours invokes the perfect degree of suffering. *Linda doesn't live here anymore.* Another two steps back in the healing process. Good job.

The town looks the same, too. Nestled in the foothills of magnificent red rocks, innocuous little mom-and-pop establishments peddle Victorian gifts, country living décor, scrapbook supplies—nothing funky or eccentric. The newsstand displays this month's issue of Cosmopolitan behind a chunk of black plastic to shield us from the shapely model's allure. While Cedar City's physical setting calls to one's sense of adventure, the collective vibe feels bleached and scoured to ensure nothing skirting the borders of decency will ever take root. Yuk.

I could shake off the repressive culture when I lived here, but after five months of enjoying the decadence of Las Vegas, this place now gives me the creeps. My innate defiance against authority yearns to rebel. I fantasize about covering myself in vulgar tattoos and shouting obscenities as I strut down Main Street with a lesbian lover—let's make her black—in our matching "Jesus Hates Me" T-shirts. It's a shame; it's beautiful here. If I could populate the town with the people from Laramie, I'd never want to leave.

His car is parked in its usual spot, and according to plan, he's left it unlocked. I dump two bags of crap in the back seat. That should be the last of it. I meant to tell him he'd better change the address for his precious *Economist* subscription because from now on I'm throwing them the fuck out.

It's weird to be in his energy. But since I am, I may as well snoop a little. I search for a morsel of evidence, some hint of what he's been up to lately, unsure of what I hope to find. Receipts? Condoms? *The Guide to Picking Up Girls, Volume II?* I'd still love to know what that was about. I rummage through his glove compartment—"glove box," as he calls it—and find, of all things, gloves. Damn! He's not this tidy. I bet he cleaned out the car just this morning, knowing I'd be in it.

Afterward I meet up with my girlfriends Michael and Becky at the bar at Applebee's. Earth-mother Becky, in her flowing skirt and Birkenstocks, is as sweet as ever. She has papers to grade, though, and stays for only a minute. Too bad. Michael is decked out in Ann Taylor from head to toe, her way of proclaiming, "I'm not from here; I just live here." She continues to struggle, I can tell. Her clothes are exquisite, but her face looks like she just had a throw-up burp.

Who could blame her? I'd be reaching for the razor blades if I were in the middle of my third divorce. She and Mona are the same age, and like Mona, her "marital dissolution" is much more complicated than mine was. They have assets to divide, a house to give up. But unlike Mona, Michael actually liked her husband. That makes it harder.

She motions for a refill and our pigtailed barmaid hurries over.

"I'm sorry, ladies, I can't serve you another drink until you order something to eat," she informs us.

"Oh, Jesus," I groan.

"Exactly," Michael murmurs.

Someone in pigtails is denying us alcohol. "You can't have more than one drink unless you order food," she explains. "Would you like to try our cheesy bacon tavern chips?"

Michael can bite that girl's head off in one chomp. "Whatever happened to separation of church and state?" she asks, as she reaches for her lighter and cigarettes.

Pippi Longstocking is all over her. "I'm sorry, ma'am. You'll have to go outside to smoke." Michael rolls her eyes in my direction. She's deliberately being a pain in the ass, and she's digging it. "Okay," she sighs, "we'll take your cheesy bacon whatever-the-hell-it-is and I'll have another vodka and cranberry."

"Certainly, ma'am."

"Make it a double," she adds, kicking me under the bar.

"We can't serve doubles, ma'am. I can give you a one-ounce pour and a side car. That's a one-ounce shot on the side. You'll have to mix it yourself."

"You can't serve doubles?" Michael shakes her head, though she knows the rules damn well. "Fine, give me the side car thing." God, she's precious. As long as it's not directed at me, bitchy people can be utterly delightful.

I want to play, too. "I'll have another Sam Adams, please."

"Ma'am, I can't serve you until you've finished that one. You can only have one beer in front of you at a time."

I raise my three-quarter empty glass. "So if I chug this, you'll bring me another?"

"Yes, ma'am."

"You want me to chug my beer before I drive all the way back to Vegas?"

"Yes, ma'am," she says, and marches away while she still can.

I turn to Michael, and though I'm no Jack Nicholson, coolly deliver my line. "I'd like an omelet, plain, and a chicken salad sandwich on wheat toast…" I need go no further. She gets it. Michael is pretty when she smiles.

I tell her about my stand-up debut three days from now.

"I can see you doing comedy," she comments, without a hint of wonder. "You're the funniest person I know." Coming from someone whose lips curl only while tormenting a poor coed over morality laws, that means a lot. I think.

§ § §

A short patch of I-15 clips the remote northwestern corner of Arizona and winds along the narrow walls of the Virgin River canyon. My drive through here earlier in the day was a steady climb through colorful cliffs and rocky crags, a scene, like so many out West, that impels me to thank God for my eyesight. Tonight I cruise downhill in the darkness, a little faster than I probably should. With both hands on the steering wheel, I maneuver the twisting pavement like a Play Station game, accumulating imaginary points with every passing mile marker.

This bit of highway that links the divergent worlds of Utah and Nevada serves as a birth canal of sorts. It was wonderful to see Becky and Michael, but it's clear they're in a world where I no longer fit; that part of my life is over. Even the twinge of nostalgia I felt in front of our old house ebbed in no time.

After twenty minutes of joyful careening, the road ejects me from the canyon into the wide open sky. Cut loose from the protective parent, I'm on my own, with infinite possibilities lying ahead.

Utah is behind me. I'm a Vegas girl now.

§ § §

That's the phone ringing inside my apartment. *Hold on, hold on, hold on!* I slip the key in the door and rush in. "Hello?"

"Linda Lou, it's Chief," says the voice on the other end. "I'm in town."

Yippee! I fire away questions one after another: Where are you staying? How long are you here for? When can we get together?

"Anything special going on this weekend?" he asks.

"Is there ever," I tell him. "You won't believe what I have in store for Sunday night."

Though I've known Chief for almost twenty years, I really don't know him very well. Sometimes I have to think hard to remember his real name. Chief's a friend of a friend who surfaces at weddings and other shindigs and who I associate with a rip-roaring good time. Like me, as the night wears on, he turns into one of those happy drunks in love with the world, and usually sometime after midnight I've settled myself on his lap with both arms wrapped around his neck. He'll be the perfect moral support for me at Boomers. I love Chief!

This is great; it's all fitting into place, I know it. Everything is perfect.

13.

Lola called first thing this morning to say she's "all in," her way of telling me she's not up for a visit today. Hate to say it, but just as well. I need the time to practice.

At church I put an extra ten dollars on the plate and begged God to please, please, give me a good hair day for Boomers tonight. At least I'm feeling thin. I should; I've been exercising like a maniac, if only to work off the adrenaline. Just sitting here on the couch right now, I bet I'm burning a million calories a minute.

I know what I'm going to wear—black pants and a cute little stretchy top I got for $7.99 at Ross Dress for Less. It's very low cut, kind of sleazy. Strategy: if the jokes suck, at least people can enjoy the cleavage. Truth is, it's the Wonderbra you should wonder about; objects are much smaller than they appear. I just know how to package them.

Everything is under control. I've rehearsed my set a hundred times, typed it out, formatted the punch lines in bullet points, wrote the bullet points out in longhand, and made a short list of my main topics: *Dad, breasts, beauty sleep, yoga, hospice. Dad, breasts, beauty sleep, yoga, hospice.* D-B-B-Y-H—what does that spell? Nothing. Forget it.

It's three o'clock. I have to be at Boomers by quarter to eight. I told Chief I'll pick him up on the corner of Harmon and Koval at seven-fifteen; that way I can avoid the Strip. I think he and his brother are staying at the Boardwalk. Anyway, that means I have to leave here by quarter to seven, which means I should be in the shower by, what, six? I ought to give myself a cushion of time, in case something happens, like… I don't know what. Okay, if I'm in the shower by six, that means I should meditate at five-thirty, which means I have to start my yoga at quarter to five. Wait, I have to eat sometime—when? And what'll I have? I can't eat anything that'll bloat me up, and certainly nothing that'll loosen me up. Sometimes I get diarrhea when I'm nervous. Oh, my God—what if I get on stage and suddenly can't control my shit like poor Little Betsy? I have to call her. Not today, though.

I have to remember to tell Marcus to introduce me as "Linda Lou." Chief started calling me Linda Lou years ago; that'll be my stage name. I don't want to be known by the last name I have now, I may decide not to keep it. I can change my name back to Blackwell, if I want. I put that in our divorce papers at the last minute, in case I don't want to spend the rest of my days as Linda Bastard-Wife. Blackwell is Chris's last name, and my kids' last name. I was Linda Blackwell for twenty-three years. Everyone back east knows me as Linda Blackwell. Or Linda Haber, my maiden name, but I can't go back to that; Linda Haber's a little girl, a cheerleader, though I still have cheerleader tendencies. I hate that term, "maiden name." Sounds queer. Not gay queer, stupid queer, like how kids used to call each other queer and it had nothing to do with gayness. At least I never meant it that way. I don't think I knew gay people were even invented until one of my aunts left her husband for a woman.

Wait, what the fuck am I doing? It's three forty-seven! I have to get on the yoga mat, eat, meditate, shower, get dressed, pick up

Chief, what else? Practice my set—duh. My set! I hate my material. Nothing's funny. It's all stupid shit. Everyone's gonna be like, why is she on stage? I'll probably forget it all anyway.

Stop that. I'm well prepared, really. I know this material; it's fine. For God's sake, this is my first time on stage—I can't expect to be Jerry Seinfeld. I mean, what's the worst that could happen?

In addition to totally forgetting my lines and losing control of bowel functions? Well, there's always bladder functions; I could have piss running down my leg as well as feces. Projectile vomiting on the people in the front row—that could happen. Or, I could suddenly develop Tourette's syndrome and randomly shout obscenities and racial slurs. That would be entertaining.

Oh, I am never, ever doing this again. Never. Ever.

Is that a blotch on my neck already?

§ § §

I feel soooo much better. Yoga is so cool—it teaches you to back away from the tension and hang out in the eye of the storm. I have to remember that tonight. That, and Dad, breasts, beauty sleep, yoga, hospice.

Set-ups and punch lines stream through my head while I shower. Tonight's big event warrants my finest facial cleansers and a new razor. I shave my legs and groom the bikini line like I'm going out on a third date with a really cute guy. Why? I have no idea.

Dad, breasts, beauty sleep, yoga, hospice.

The mirror says I look good. Yep, face looks good…ass looks good…hair looks okay…This blouse is hot! If only the boys from my old neighborhood could see me now. Maybe Linda Haber was a member of the Itty Bitty Titty Committee, but Linda Lou has a dynamite rack.

Dad, breasts, beauty sleep, yoga, hospice.

"Chief? Linda Lou here. How'd the football go today?" I could give a crap about football. "Good. I'm leaving my apartment. Give me, like, twenty minutes. Yeah, Koval and Harmon. In front of the garage to the Aladdin. Okay. See ya."

Dad, breasts, beauty sleep, yoga, hospice.

§ § §

Fake it till you make it. I'm not nearly as in control as I'm pretending to be. I want to cry. And throw up. I can't wait for this to be over. Never again. Ever.

I head west on the 215 like I'm driving myself to prison. The radio is off; I can't handle any distractions, not on top of the chaos going on in my head. *Shhhhh...*

After passing through the airport tunnel, I slow down as I approach the light at Tropicana. Though traffic's not too bad in Las Vegas on a Sunday night, this corner always seems to be backed up. The delay gives me a chance to practice some yoga breathing. I happen to look up to my left. Directly above me a billboard for Lance Burton displays an image of the performer and an endorsement, "Best I've ever seen—Johnny Carson."

It's a sign. Well, duh, it is a sign; it's a billboard. But it's a *sign*! I sent my jokes to Johnny Carson when I was a kid! Holy shit, this is a goddamn sign. I can't take my eyes off it. For once I wish the light would stay red just a little while longer.

Best I've ever seen. I'll be fine! I will deliver my set no problem. That's all I want—just to get through it. And I will! Now, does this mean I should do my Captain Hook joke?

Chief is in his designated position on the corner, grinning at God knows what.

"Linda Loooooo…" he hoots, plopping into the passenger's seat. He's half in the bag. Or at least getting there.

"Great to see you, Chief!" I present my right cheek so he doesn't mess up my lipstick. "It's been a long time. Couple of years, anyway."

"You're lookin' good," he says, eyeing the Vegas frontage I've put together for the occasion.

"You, too!" Chief looks like a cute version of Alfred E. Newman. He's adorable.

"So, you all ready?" he asks. "You doin' okay?"

"I am ready to jump out of my fucking skin, Chief. But, yeah, I'm doing fine."

Dad, breasts, beauty sleep, yoga, hospice.

§ § §

It's early, and already there's a decent crowd here at Boomers.

"What can I get you, Linda Lou?" Chief asks.

"Just a club soda."

"You sure?" He seems disappointed.

"Yeah. I need every single brain cell I have right now." I poke his arm. "Just have a big-ass beer waiting for me when I get off that stage."

Chief gets my soda and orders a Jack and Coke for himself and follows me to the back room. We claim a table big enough for the others I expect to be coming to see me. "Linda's going to be a stand-up comic!" Mona announced at our divorce support meeting Tuesday. I could have killed her, but actually it will be nice to have them here.

There she is now, with Sanjay, Leticia, and Sharon. I motion and they head over.

"Lin-duhhhh!" Mona rushes to give me a hug. "So, are you

excited?"

"A little too excited." My friends smile widely with anticipation and offer words of encouragement. I introduce everyone to Chief, and realize I'm barely in the room. *Dad, breasts, beauty sleep, yoga, hospice.* I have to go over my set—*what about* Dad, breasts, beauty sleep, yoga, hospice? I'm starting to forget.

"You guys, I need to go out and review my notes. Do you mind?" I don't care if they do. "I'll be back. Save my seat."

I sit on a banquette out in the bar area and pull my notes from my pocketbook. Shit. It's too dark in here; I can't see a damned thing. Rummaging through my bag I realize I've left my reading glasses on the coffee table at home. *Come on, don't freak. Johnny Carson said you're the best he's ever seen.* Staring at the blur on the pages, I try to make out what I'd typed up earlier. Where are my handwritten bullets? They might be bigger.

"So, are you excited about your comedy debut?" Marcus stands over me.

Is he crazy? "Do you not see the terror etched into my face?"

"You'll be fine. You'll be fourth in the lineup, after Tony P."

"Okay." Good, I have to sit through only three people before I get up. "Um, can you introduce me as Linda Lou?"

"Yup," Marcus says, making a note on a yellow pad.

"And, um, after you introduce me, can you hand me the microphone? I mean, don't put it back in the stand. I don't really know how to work it. Is that okay? Can you just hand it to me?"

He pats my shoulder. "Sure thing, Linda Lou."

§ § §

I have no idea what I'm laughing at. Tony P. is getting a good response, and I just laugh along with the rest of the crowd. Every once in a while I take a sip of my drink and smile at the people at my table. They see my physical presence, but they have no idea how very far away I am from them. I'm up next. Deep breathing. Eye of the storm. Dad, breasts, beauty sleep, yoga, hospice.

"Thank you! That's my time!" And that's the end of Tony P. I sit erect on the edge of my seat flashing the fakest of smiles. Holy fucking shit. Please God, let me get through this in one piece.

After Tony P. exits the stage Marcus returns to his emcee duties. "I have a real treat for you tonight. Our next comic is a lovely lady who's making her comedy debut, right here at Boomers. Please give a big welcome to the beautiful Miss Linda Lou!"

Thank you, Marcus, for that nice introduction. People are clapping. *For me.* I rise and feign confidence as I stroll to the front of the room. Shoulders back and down, head high, lead with the sternum. Marcus remembers to hand me the mic. He looks me in the eye and with the kindest smile anyone has given me in my whole entire life, whispers, "Have fun." *Oh, God bless you.*

"Thank you, gee, thanks," I say to the crowd. The light shines in my face, I see only shadowy formations out there. *Keep going. Eye of the storm.* "Hi, everyone. I'm Linda Lou. I won't bother you with a last name because, well, it changes with every husband." Mild response. Deep breath. "You know, they say you marry a man like your father, but honestly, I'm not that attracted to overweight bus drivers." Big laugh. *Okay, you're in.*

This is freaking surreal. I'm like, out of body. Am I shaking? Where the hell am I? Somehow words continue to pour from my mouth. To me, I sound like Charlie Brown's teacher—"Waahh, wahhh, waahhh...breasts...Waahh, wahhh...beauty sleep..." People are laughing, though. *People are laughing.* This is exactly what was supposed to happen. More words...I can't tell—did they go for my Barnes and Noble joke? Doesn't matter, I'm having my own experience. What's after yoga again? Oh, hospice.

"I'm a hospice volunteer. Yeah, I became a hospice volunteer because…I'm not good with long-term relationships." Huge laugh. Couple more lines, then I'm gonna quit while I'm ahead. I have to get off this stage.

"Thank you so much! I'm Linda Lou!"

I hear people clap, and I think I hear woo-ing and whistling. *Thank God, thank God, thank God.* Marcus takes the mic from me and says, "Nice job" before addressing the audience. "How about that? Her first time ever! Once again, give it up for Linda Lou!" I'm aware of more clapping as I float back to my table. Mona stands to give me another big hug. "You were great!" she says, ever the proud Jewish mother. The others look at me, beaming.

Chief places a twenty-ounce draft in front of me. "Good job, Linda Lou."

I have no idea what kind of beer it is; it's beer and that's all that matters. I use both hands to raise the heavy glass to my lips—one alone would be way too shaky—and take a big victory swig. As I breathe through the tremors of the aftershock, I start to gain some presence of mind and realize *I did it.* And I never have to do it again. Ever.

Gradually my physical being returns to the room and I can actually see the people at my table. I now return their kind sentiments with a smile that's sincerely appreciative instead of the clenched expression I've held so far tonight. Every time we make eye contact, Mona showers praise in a voice that has absolutely no regard for the comic in the spotlight at the moment. How lucky I am to have these people from my group, and to think that six months ago I didn't even know them. Leticia, the beautiful Latin temptress. *"Oh, Leen-da,* you were so good," she says. Sweet Sharon, who will some-day emerge from her protective shell. And Sanjay, where is he from again? India? Pakistan? I think he's a retired physician. Always so serious. I'm surprised to see him here.

And Chief! How cute is he? Look at the rugby player sip his drink with his pinkie up in the air. I think we should check out the *ghostbar,* the lounge at the Palms, later. I've been dying to go there, but not by myself. I can solo it in Irish pubs and the Railhead, but I wouldn't hang out alone at an ultralounge. Especially not in this blouse—people might think I'm a hooker.

I bask in the exhilaration of my accomplishment and pretend to take in the next couple of comics while I replay my performance in my head. *Dad, breasts…*shit, I totally left out one of my favorite Victoria's Secret lines. Oh, well—no one knows but me.

By the time the headliner takes the stage, I'm somewhat able to direct my attention outside my own little world. I've seen this guy before; his name is Manny. He has two brothers who look exactly like him—well, I think, anyway—and no doubt I've called them all "Manny" at some point. He does a hilarious impression of Martin Luther King placing an order at the drive-thru window at McDonald's and has a confident stage presence I can only hope to achieve someday. Except I'm never doing this again. Once Manny finishes his set, Marcus returns to address us one last time. As usual, he thanks the crowd and rattles off the names of all the comics who performed tonight, and when I hear mine midway through the list, the adrenaline starts to resurge. *I did it.*

The lights come up and I rise from my seat. In addition to my friends, a few other people wait to have a word with me. Smelly Dick Boy, the Andrew Dice Clay wannabe, gets to me first and gives my left shoulder a little rub. "Nice set, baby."

"Thank you, really. Thank you so much," I say, assuming he's referring to my performance. He's nice. I should feel bad for naming him Smelly Dick Boy.

An attractive black woman wearing a colorful African print caftan bustles up to us. "Linda Lou, I want you on my stage!" she commands. It's odd to hear someone other than Chief call me Linda Lou.

Wait, what the hell is she talking about?

"I'm Cozy Stone. I book talent for showcases around town."

So what does she want with *me?*

"Here, write down your phone number." She thrusts a pen and appointment book in my face. "It's hard to find female comics, and it's almost impossible to find clean comics, and honey, you're both. I want you on my stage."

Back in William S. Hackett Junior High School, little Linda Haber never said no to big girls like this one. Even though I'm quite sure this woman is not harassing me, I obediently give her my contact information as if I'm handing over my bus money. "Thank you," I say. For what, I don't know.

"Thank *you!*" she insists. "Honey, you were wonderful. I'll be in touch with you soon."

I don't know what exactly just went on, but I have a feeling I will, in fact, have to do this again. So much for never, ever.

§ § §

There's no line at the *ghostbar*, maybe because it's Sunday or maybe it's still early—not yet eleven o'clock. Chief insists on paying the cover charge and I don't put up much of a fight. I'm almost afraid to look at my money situation these days, but I'm not about to concern myself with that now. I'm still flying high from my set at Boomers, and thinking of my checkbook would be a definite buzz kill. Chief hands a twenty to the pretty cashier, who in turn directs us to an elevator that will take us to the fifty-fifth floor of the Palms Casino Resort.

The scene is just what I imagined—floor-to-ceiling windows, filtered blue lighting, futuristic metallic and chrome decor. A pulsing, yet non-intrusive beat adds to the vibe. House music? Hip-hop? Techno? Honestly, I don't know the difference—how cool am I? Model-quality waitresses—all legs, tits, teeth, and hair—provide bottle service to clusters of stylish partiers relaxing on silver sofas. People are dressed to impress, but their expressions lack pretension. I like that. We're not the oldest ones here, either. I really like that.

Chief beats me to the bar and returns with a Newcastle and yet another Jack and Coke for himself. "You should have let me get the drinks," I tell him.

He'll have no part of that. "No, no, Linda Lou. You're the star tonight. Cheers."

Burly bouncers wearing dark suits and lots of hair gel survey the crowd from their assigned posts throughout the room. Their demeanor seems cordial, not predatory like the asshole security guards you see at rock shows. One of them stops us on our way out to the rooftop patio off the lounge area. "Let me pour that into a plastic cup for you," he says, taking my beer bottle. "Here you go, ma'am."

Ma'am? Too happy to be annoyed, I smile graciously.

It's early November and the air is still warm enough to be outside at night without a jacket. "Wow!" Chief and I react simultaneously to the stunning view of the city before us. "Look!" he says. Beyond the glittering lights of the Strip about eight planes line up in the eastern sky, awaiting their turn to land. They appear to be at eye level. As we stand in silence, taking it all in, a rush of gratitude overcomes me. I could burst into tears, I am so overwhelmed with thanks. Thanks for not only getting through my set, but for actually doing pretty well. For the people who came to see me, for a decent hair day, for the Johnny Carson sign.

I'm feeling shaky again. "I did it, Chief."

He rests his forearm on my shoulder. "Linda Lou, I have to say, I was nervous for you tonight. I mean, you were always a sweetheart, but…" He checks his words before continuing. "I never really thought you were that funny."

I have to laugh. "That makes two of us." But maybe Linda Blackwell, the one Chief used to party with, wasn't that funny. Maybe Linda Lou is.

"You did good, though," he says. "You did really good."

A few feet away a blonde in a lime green halter delights in jumping on a transparent acrylic slab built into the floor. This section of the patio hangs away from the building, fifty-five stories above the pool area. Her friend—no, maybe it's her mother—is not so daring. A woman who looks like a middle-aged Skipper doll tentatively places one platformed sandal on the glass as if she might fall through any second.

"Britney Spears was dancing on that Friday night," I tell Chief. I'm so in-the-know. Our newspaper has the best celebrity gossip.

Chief and I wait for them to move on before we check it out for ourselves. "Can't really see anything at night," I say, peering into the darkness below. I lightly bounce on the thing a few times. "It's a miracle I'm not afraid of heights, considering all my other phobias."

"You still afraid of birds?"

I shudder. "Oh, my *God*, yes!" So dramatic, I am. "Birds, pictures of Jesus, fake fingernails..."

"Why birds?" he asks, as if certainly everyone is afraid of pictures of Jesus and fake fingernails.

"They could fly into my head, Chief!" *Duh.* "If I see birds on the sidewalk, I have to jiggle my keys or stamp my feet or clear my throat so they fly away. Isn't that queer?" *Queer.* "I think it's a germ thing. God only knows the infestation under all those feathers. Same with long, fake fingernails. I could be starving to death, but if I get a waitress with fake fingernails, I swear, I can't eat. Think of the crap that gets stuck under those things." I know the look Chief is giving me—it's the same "God, she's crazy" look that I get from Lola. And like Lola, he waits for more. "Pictures of Jesus…not related to germs," I add. "That's something different."

Chief shakes his head. "I'm learning things tonight, Linda Lou. See? I never knew you were funny and I never knew you were such a nut."

I give him a poke. "Well, now you know. After all these years."

A couch on the south side of the patio opens up and we seize the opportunity. I let out a big "Aaaah…" as I sit back, releasing what I hope is the last bit of nervous energy. As we catch up on our mutual friends, I realize how nice it is to be conversing with a person I actually know, instead of hanging out by myself and hoping somebody decent will start talking to me. Chief's the perfect drinking buddy. I can enjoy his company—and I really do—without having to worry about him putting the moves on me. And the best part is, Chief is no longer just a friend-of-a-friend. As of tonight, he's *my* friend.

"How are your kids doing? How old are they now?" he asks.

I love talking about my babies. "Christopher's twenty-five and Courtney's twenty-four."

"No—how can that be? Remember them serving beers to us at parties? Little Courtney pumping the keg…Jesus."

"Connor will be five the day after Christmas. Hopefully he's not pumping kegs."

"I keep forgetting you're a grandma," Chief says.

"Granny," I correct him. "He calls me Granny." The thought of Connor's little voice pulls at my heart. "That kid is so *cute*," I gush. "I miss him so much. I miss them all. I can't wait to see them next month when I go back for the holidays."

"Do you think you'll ever move back to Albany?"

"No! I love it here. The sunshine, the warmth…it's where I'm supposed to be." I take note of both the swiftness of my answer and the passion behind my response.

"What about Chris? Do you ever see him?"

"Yeah, I usually stay at Courtney's house and he stops in. He's fine. I love Chris; I would never say anything bad about him. Unlike the other ex, that bastard."

"I never met him. But, yeah, Chris was a good guy."

"What about you, do you ever see Katie?" I don't know how Chief managed to find a wife who looked exactly like him.

He gazes off into the lights. "No. We weren't married that long. You know how it is. When you don't have kids, there's no reason to see each other."

There's no reason to see each other. The thought that I may never see B.H. again is another one that pulls at my heart.

Chief's eyes are starting to cross. If he was half lit when I picked him up, at this point he's fully ignited. Between the Jack and Cokes and his thick Long Island accent, I understand maybe every third word he mumbles. "Whaa, whaa, whaa…Linda Lou," is about all I can decipher.

"C'mon, Chief, let's go."

The drive down the Strip at 2 a.m. is a breeze. We now look up at the lights we oversaw from the rooftop of the Palms. What a place this is. I really do love it here.

I pull over to the entrance to the Boardwalk. "Chief, it's been great hanging out with you again. I'm so glad you were there to support me tonight." I lean over to give him a peck, and what does he do but slip me the tongue. Boys will be boys. I gently pull away, praying I don't seem rude, though given his condition, odds are he'll never remember. Things are improving, anyway—at the end of the night I'd rather be kissed by someone drunk than have him call me a fucking bitch.

Back home I decompress by clicking through the late-night cable offerings. Nothing's worth watching; I should go to bed. I pick a spiritual book off the shelf and randomly select a page, as I sometimes do, for a bit of inspiration to mull over before I go to sleep. A sentence jumps out at me: *When you truly understand, there is nothing to forgive.*

Whatever.

14.

I'm on a roll; I'm on a freaking roll! The training manager from the Hard Rock called this morning to see if I could come in for an interview today. I completed an online application last week, swearing my head off as usual, and figured it would end up in the cyber black hole along with the rest of them, but no. This is awesome.

Driving to my interview, I follow last night's route to Boomers. Today as I cruise along the 215, I rehearse lines of a different sort.

My training philosophy? *I believe an effective training program begins with clearly defined performance standards. Once the performance standards are in place, then you conduct a needs assessment to determine... blah, blah...* Okay, I have that script down.

My strengths and weaknesses? *As far as strengths go, I'm experienced in all aspects of the training process, with particular expertise in instructional design and training delivery. Evaluating training is always a challenge, don't you think? Tell me, how do you measure training effectiveness here at the Hard Rock?* That's good. Sounds like I know what I'm talking about, and by asking a question, maybe we'll never get around to my weaknesses.

My weaknesses! *Well, to begin, my work ethic is...lackluster. I have absolutely no career aspirations. I work only because I have to, and quite frankly, I was never happier than when I was a spoiled faculty wife teaching a few yoga classes between pedicures and lunches with my girlfriends. And, I have major problems with authority.* I can't imagine why no one's hired me yet.

I'm well prepared for this and I look good, I think. Dark gray pants, black top, and a black jacket—that should work. I tried to come up with something youthful and cool-looking, yet professional. Can't go wrong in New York City black. Good thing I dyed my hair last week. Gray roots—not hip. Can't work at the Hard Rock looking like that.

Passing through the airport tunnel, I look forward to seeing the billboard for Lance Burton again while I wait for the light at Tropicana. But...what the hell? Today it's animated. Johnny Carson's *"Best I've ever seen"* quotation is now one of many; it flashes for only a few seconds before the next accolade displays. Last night I stared at his words for at least a whole minute, I'm sure of that. Weird.

I strut into the Hard Rock Hotel and Casino with the same confidence as my walk to the stage at Boomers last night. Photographs of music icons line the walls from the parking garage to the casino area, and I pause to study a picture of a young Jackson Browne sitting barefoot on the steps of an old bus. God, he's cute. How I'd stare into those eyes on his Late for the Sky album. I'm glad Christopher's middle name is Jackson. He probably thinks it's queer. *Queer.*

A petite college-aged girl approaches me. "Excuse me," she says. "Where's Mr. Lucky's?" My vacuous look tells her I have no idea who Mr. Lucky is, and she immediately adds, "Oh, I'm sorry. I thought you worked here."

This happens all the time—wherever I go, people ask me questions because they think I work there. I'll be shopping in a store in jeans with my pocketbook slung over my shoulder and invariably someone will ask me where the dressing rooms are. A few weeks ago, as Mona and I waited at the hostess station at Marie Callenders, a couple came up to me and said, "Two. Non-smoking." I must carry myself with an air of authority. It's the good posture from yoga, I bet.

I seem to hit it off right away with the training manager, Jeremy. Usually you know within the first minute or so if the rest of the interview will progress well, and sometimes, no matter how well-qualified you are, you find yourself in front of someone who simply doesn't like your stinkin' looks. The woman who interviewed me at the Bellagio last month certainly didn't. Maybe she picked up my mental mocking of her stuck-in-the-eighties hairdo, with the curly bangs that sat on her forehead like a goddamn bird's nest. Lucky for me, Jeremy seems to like my looks. I like his—I can't resist a cute young guy in a ponytail. He asks intelligent questions, which thrills me to no end, and he actually seems to understand my answers. Jeremy agrees that evaluating training effectiveness is a major challenge, and he's honest enough to admit he's yet to come up with a reliable measuring system. We talk and laugh, and if this were a first date I'd ever so subtly undo my top button. Maybe I will anyway.

I gaze up at the photo of Lou Reed above Jeremy's bookcase. Bird's Nest Girl decorated her office with those stupid motivational prints you see. Like I'm supposed to be inspired by a picture of sky-divers holding hands in the air with the caption, "Success through teamwork." Puke.

Yes, I can definitely see myself working here.

§ § §

Three voicemail messages wait for me when I get home. <*Beep*> Jeremy wants to know if I can come back tomorrow afternoon to meet with the director of human resources. Yes! <*Beep*> The volunteer coordinator at the hospice says Lola was admitted to the inpatient unit this morning. I'm surprised; Lola said she wasn't feeling well yesterday, but she didn't sound that bad. I'll check on her tomorrow. *<Beep>* Cozy Stone wants to know if I'm available December 3 to do a set at Tailspins, whatever that is.

Good news, bad news, and Cozy's message is actually good news, too. I should be happy she liked me enough to want to book me on one of her stages. Maybe next time the experience won't be as traumatic. I hope.

I check my email and see that Wendy VonDerLinn, who's married to my dear friend Bob from GE, sent a message to me and the rest of the old gang, his partners in corporate impropriety. Oh, no... Bob's been diagnosed with "stage four squamous cell carcinoma." They found the primary site of the cancer at the base of the tongue and it's metastasized to the lymph nodes on both sides of his neck. He starts radiation treatments at Sloan Kettering on Wednesday. She'll keep us posted as they know more. Fuck.

Two good messages, two bad. The balance of the universe.

§ § §

For the third time in as many days, I wait for the light at Tropicana and stare up at my billboard. Again, it's animated. Am I going crazy? Was it, in fact, flashing Sunday night as I sat here on my way to Boomers? Or have I gotten to the point where I see only what I want to see?

The human resources manager is nice—her name is Karen—and like Jeremy, she knows her stuff. She appears to be a few years older than me, which is good. I never imagined that age discrimination could actually pertain to me—at forty-six, I'm hardly an old fart—but you never know in a youth-oriented place like the Hard Rock. Vegas has its own set of employment laws. That's why there are no cocktail waitresses with A cups.

Today's meeting is clearly one of those courtesy interviews they put you through just so other people in the company can get a look at you before you're hired. That's okay. I enjoy chatting with Karen. As we wrap up, Jeremy pops his head in.

"How's it going?" he asks.

"Great!" we say, in unison. Good, she thinks it's going well, too.

"Did you ask about the presentation?" Jeremy directs his question to Karen.

"No, not yet."

He turns to me. "We were wondering if you could present a twenty-minute mock training session on a topic related to customer service, whatever you want. I'm hoping a few people from other departments will attend, too, if that's okay."

"Sure, I'd love to," I tell him.

"Great. Let me coordinate everyone's schedule and I'll let you know when I come up with a date. I'm targeting early next week. Does that work for you?"

"Next week is fine." Tomorrow is fine. I'll do it right now.

"Okay, then. I'll be holding a class myself a week from Friday. I'd also like you to sit in on that, if you're available."

Am I ever! Heading back to the parking garage, I practically dance along the main walkway around the perimeter of the casino floor, my steps in synch with the beat of a song I'm familiar with, but I can't place the artist. Coldplay, is it? I think so. I really don't know. Who are the White Stripes anyway? I'm going to have to get with it.

Oh, I have such a *good* feeling—this is so in the bag. They wouldn't have me do a presentation and sit in on Jeremy's training if I weren't a serious candidate. To think I was this close to selling graves. And timeshares! Oh, my God, I actually looked at the school district's website to be a substitute—can you imagine? I get the impression Jeremy wants to fill the position ASAP, which is perfect. I need a paycheck.

Everything is perfect; life unfolds in divine order. I have to remember that. Last month I was sure nothing could be better than working at the Bellagio, and I was bummed when that didn't work out. Now the Bellagio can kiss my ass—I'd much rather work for Jeremy and his ponytail than Bird's Nest Girl who, by the way, took a personal phone call right in the middle of my interview. The Hard Rock is *so* me. I'm much more rock and roll than classy. I probably shouldn't admit that, but it's true.

On my way home I stop at the hospice to see Lola. I'm flying high, and really should tone down the mood a bit; after all, people are dying around here. I check the board in the break room to see where they've put her. My favorite nurse, Jerry with the little boy's face, thrusts a plate of chocolate chip cookies in front of me. "Here," he says, "Bernadette made these."

"No thanks, I just ate." I feel bad about lying, but I can't eat food from just anybody's kitchen. What if they let their cats walk all over the counter tops? Or, they could pet their dog or blow their nose and then put their filthy hands right back in the cookie dough. Plus, I cannot stand Bernadette. She's the hospice chaplain, and she walks around the place like God himself appointed her to the position. Now *there's* someone who doesn't like my stinkin' looks; she can probably tell I don't buy into her whole Jesus scene. On my way to Lola's room I pass the bitch and give her a super-warm "hello," if only to annoy her.

Lola's awake, propped up in bed and staring at the television, which is not turned on. I take a few steps into the room and stop abruptly, dramatically placing my hands on my hips. "What do you call this?" I ask, enunciating my words and frowning in pretend exasperation.

Her eyes light up and she breaks into a smile I can feel in my heart. *I got Lola to smile!* I pull a chair to the side of her bed. "What's goin' on?"

She waves a hand in the air at the bother of it all, her little finger catching on a tube from her oxygen. "I had trouble breathing so they put me in here for a few days." She looks good, though her voice seems a bit weakened.

"Can I get you anything?"

"No, dear. I'm fine. Don't you look nice."

"Thanks. I just had an interview at the Hard Rock."

Her eyebrows crowd together. Now there's the face I know and love.

"It's a hotel and casino," I explain. "With a rock-and-roll theme."

She nods. I expected a frown of disapproval.

"So you were deep in thought when I came in," I say.

"I was thinking about you, dear. I was thinking about that book."

"What book is that?"

"Your husband's book. For picking up girls."

"Oooh. *That* book." I place my hand on top of hers. "What about it?"

"You said it yourself. You said that was the one thing you wouldn't put up with."

"That's right. I put up with his drinking and all the crap that went along with it, but other women? No." This is not what I expected to talk about today. "I'll never understand it, Lola. It's not like he's a ladies' man or anything, believe me..."

She cuts me off. "No, you *don't* understand." Lola has something up her sleeve, and she's clearly digging the fact that she's onto something I'm not. "Don't you see, dear? The book got you out of his way."

"Out of his way?" She doesn't try to elaborate. It's starting to sink in. I was what stood between him and his vices. He'd been hungering for an escape route for a long time, and infidelity would be a certain deal breaker.

"You think he planted the book for me to find? On purpose?"

Lola nods, proud to have cracked the case.

"Yeah," I say. "I think you're right." I believe I've heard the truth, but I can't fully process it right now. I pat her hand twice. "Hey, guess what I did Sunday night."

15.

The mock training session I did for the folks at the Hard Rock kicked ass. Both Jeremy and Karen had the highest praise for my presentation skills, and when the general manager stopped in afterward, everyone told him what a great trainer I am. The next morning I observed Jeremy's class on loss prevention. Just as I imagined, he has a nice, down-to-earth training style. Afterward he asked for a list of references and said he'd get back to me later that afternoon.

That was six weeks ago.

Evidently the powers that be, whoever those fuckers are, decided to cut the training department's budget for the coming year. Jeremy said his hands are tied until they're sure the position will, in fact, be funded. I want to believe him. At first I wondered if the funding issue may have been a fabrication—an easy out—but he seemed sincerely apologetic, and I should remember that not everyone is looking to escape from me.

So I'm going to be a substitute teacher after all. What a pain in the ass this has been, between the online interest form, three-page application and cash layouts, one after the other—eighty-five dollars for a license, twenty bucks for fingerprints, thirty-five for the FBI background check, and I forget how much it cost to get my official college transcripts. And for some reason, though all my classes posted to my records, my master's degree itself never did. So now, twelve years after the fact, I face a nightmare of red tape to straighten that mess out. The interview, however, was a breeze since I'm lucky enough to have a warm body. The school district is so short-staffed, as long as you meet the educational requirements and no felonies of a lewd or heinous nature surface in the background check, I think they'd greenlight pretty much anyone.

After completing the selection process, I sat through two full days of training—paid, thank God. Of course, they gave us more paperwork to fill out. I signed up to be placed in the middle schools, figuring twelve-year-olds should definitely be toilet trained and I'd be bigger than most of them.

Lucky for the kids, the other fifty people in the auditorium seemed positive and enthusiastic. Quite a few of them are "moms" returning to the workforce, excited to be on the same schedule as their children. That's why Mona started subbing years ago. They all seemed nice enough, way nicer than me and certainly more fresh-faced since I was out until after 12:30 the night before partying with a zydeco band at the Orleans casino.

The trainers told us how to accept and decline assignments, where to look if you can't find the lesson plan the real teacher was supposed to leave for you, and what to do during a school lockdown. A school goes in lockdown mode when there's an immediate threat of danger, like when a crazed gunman is in the neighborhood. It's an absolutely horrifying practice that requires us to contain the kids in the classroom and no one's allowed to leave, even if the bell rings. I picture myself trapped with thirty-five hyperactive seventh-graders while SWAT teams scramble from the rooftops. That's enough to launch a personal crusade for non-violence.

The module on classroom management seemed kind of interesting. One of the trainers demonstrated the "stare and nod" technique she uses to regain control of the class when she can't get the students to shut the hell up. They also talked about the different medications children are on these days and I have to wonder, where were all these crazy kids when I was in school?

They told us we should never be alone with a student in the classroom; we have to move to an open doorway or talk out in the hall. And we can never, ever touch them, even to give them a hug. That's probably for the better; I still have flashbacks of nearly suffocating in my fourth-grade teacher's floral-scented bosom.

So I'll be all set up in the system and ready to start the first day back from Christmas vacation, I mean, "winter break." Each day between 6 a.m. and 9 p.m. I'll get a computer-generated call informing me of open assignments. I can't wait to be earning a big ninety dollars a day—fifteen dollars an hour. I think I was in my twenties the last time I saw that kind of money. Yippee. While the smiling image on my Nevada driver's license reflects the fun I had with my new friends at the DMV, the expression on my laminated Clark County School District photo ID—which cost me another fifteen dollars—reveals a blend of resignation and bewilderment.

I'm trying to look on the bright side: I won't be selling timeshares or cemetery plots, and at least I'll have a little income. Oh, who am I kidding? I hate looking on the bright side, just as I hate compromising and keeping an open mind. With any of them, I know that ultimately I'm not getting my way.

What was all that crap I was saying about the divine order of the universe? Everything is unfolding perfectly? Yeah, right.

§ § §

Wendy VonDerLinn's been good about sending Bob's GE buddies regular updates on his condition. Three days a week they drive to Sloan Kettering for his radiation treatments, and I guess Bob lies around the rest of the time trying to regain his strength. He can't eat because they're directing the radiation to his throat; he has to pour some kind of formula into a feeding tube for nourishment. Bob's lost almost thirty pounds already. He can't speak now, either, and Wendy said that's the saddest part, the silence. The prognosis is good, thank God, and if I know Bob, he's amassing a collection of anecdotes in his head, preparing for the day he'll entertain us with every unsavory detail of his experience with cancer.

I picture the two of them holding hands in doctors' offices and radiology waiting areas, a united front against the evil enemy. Though my heart breaks for them, there's an ugly side of me that seethes with jealousy. I think of Bastard Husband's heart attack scare a few months ago, that night after the Denis Leary movie. As he lay connected to monitors in the curtained stall in the ER, I hounded the overworked residents and nursing staff for updates on the status of blood work and EKG results, demanding their assessment of his condition. The situation put us on the same side for a mere eighteen hours, and once he was discharged, my role shifted from advocate back to adversary. Whereas cancer seems to afford Bob and Wendy a renewed appreciation for each other, my husband's disease has destroyed our relationship. Unlike Wendy, I am not my husband's rock. I am the enemy.

It *is* a disease, I'm starting to learn. I found a book called *The Addictive Personality* that reads like his autobiography; I recognize so much of the behavior. Addiction is a disease of the brain, it says, and he can't help it any more than Bob can help having cancer. I feel a sense of remorse for all the times my frustration snarled into condescension. "You're a bright person," I'd say, my tone oozing with contempt. "Figure it out. If you don't lift the bottle to your mouth, then we don't have a problem, do we?" But I can see it's not that simple, and my heart is beginning to open to him. When I meditate on the affirmation, *I am sensitive to the needs of others*, the same message comes to me every time: He needs love.

When you truly understand, there is nothing to forgive.

So on top of the disappointment of not getting the job at the Hard Rock, the prospect of having to sub, my concern for Bob's health and my renewed compassion for Bastard Husband, Lola's condition has been steadily deteriorating. She's been back in the inpatient unit for about a week now. I stopped to see her last night on my way to do a set at Boomers. She was out of it; one of the aides told me she'd been sleeping most of the day. I sat and held her hand, but the lines from my act kept intruding on my prayers, so I stayed for only a few minutes. I was afraid if I sent God mixed messages, Lola could wake up with giant boobs.

My comedy is the bright spot in my life, although I can't say I actually enjoy it. I'm still neurotic as hell and spend the whole day practicing and meditating and lighting candles. I did well last week at the Tailspin; quite a few people said they couldn't believe it was only my second time on stage. The slutty blouses seem to go over well. I bought a few more since Cozy says she has a few gigs lined up for January.

It's a miracle I can be funny, considering I've been so down lately. Maybe all comics feel that way and sometimes you just have to fake it. I admit that hanging out at the hospice before your set is probably not the best way to maintain a cheery persona. I'll have to remember that.

§ § §

"Linda? It's Debbie." The volunteer coordinator. *Shit. Lola died.* "I want to tell you, Bernadette got ahold of me this morning. Were you visiting with Lola last night?"

"Yes, is she okay?" I ask.

"She's hanging in there. No, Bernadette...well, you know how she is... she told me you were wearing something inappropriate, with a plunging neckline."

Oh, for Christsake. "Yeah, I was on my way to do stand-up. That's how I dress. Breasts are part of my act." Goddamn that Bernadette.

"Well, don't worry about it. I told her I'd talk to you." Debbie giggles. "I don't think she likes you."

"No shit."

"She said you 'sashay' around here..."

"*I sashay???*"

"And she's afraid that the patients' wives might not appreciate your being around their husbands. I told her you do yoga and that's just the way you walk."

We both burst out laughing.

"Hey, there's an envelope here for you," she says.

"What is it, a letter of termination?" Jesus, if I get fired from a volunteer job, there's very little hope of getting one that actually pays.

"Oh, no! Don't worry, I told Bernadette you're the best volunteer I have. No, I think one of the patient's visitors left it for you at the front desk."

I tell her to go ahead and open it.

"It's a poem," she says, "from Frank...I can't read the last name."

"I know who he is. We talked in the courtyard Saturday afternoon. His mother was in room fourteen."

"Well, that was nice of him. See? Everybody loves you. Don't worry about old Bernadette."

Before we hang up, I thank Debbie for her understanding and promise I'll never wear my sleazy blouses to the hospice again. And although I can't help the way I walk, she can assure Bernadette I'm not trying to steal anyone's gravely ill husband.

A bit annoyed, I sit and fume for a minute and then realize, somebody wrote a poem for *me*. That's so nice. I imagine it reads,

> "Roses are red.
> Violets are blue.
> People dying in bed
> Have the hots for you."

16.

"Hello, Linda? It's Dolores."

Whoa. I know only one Dolores—his mother. "I'm calling to wish you Merry Christmas," she says.

I try to disguise my shock with graciousness. "Dolores! How nice to hear from you." I mean it; she's a lovely woman. Proper. We stayed at her farmhouse during the holidays two years ago when he took me to New Zealand to meet his family. It's been a while since I've spoken with her, I don't know how long.

She asks how I like living in Las Vegas and if I've found a job yet. "I love it!" I gush, and then try to put a positive spin on my pathetic job search activities. "I'm going to substitute in the middle schools until I find something in my field."

"I didn't know you're a teacher," she says.

"Me neither," I reply, and leave it at that. Eventually we address the elephant in the room, Bastard Son. I mention I haven't heard from him since he moved back to Utah.

"Oh, no," she corrects me. "No, he's been living in Las Vegas. Where did I..." After some shuffling on the other side of the world, Dolores reads off the name and address of an apartment complex, which I capture on the envelope of my cable bill. "He stays at a motel near the university when he's teaching, but I believe he's been in Las

Vegas since the end of the semester." *Se-may-stah*, she pronounces it. I miss that accent.

Though I realize the gesture is unnecessary, I want to offer an explanation or apology of sorts. "Dolores, I'm so sorry that things didn't work out. I really love him, you know. But the drinking... I couldn't take it anymore."

"I understand," she says. Of course she does; no doubt his drunken antics haven't been limited to the northern hemisphere. "No, you have to go on with your life, dear. Let him go."

Let him go? Like tossing old food from the refrigerator? *Get rid of that crap. You don't need it anymore.* Go on with my life? Those are not the words I want to hear. *You're his mother, goddamn it! Make him behave! Take the belt to him if you have to!* But I suspect Dolores, too, has thrown her hands in the air, and a long time ago.

We chat over topics of an inconsequential nature. I tell her I loved the movie *Whale Rider* and I bet the weather down there is starting to get nice with the beginning of summer. As the conversation nears a close, we wish each other happy holidays and it almost panics me to realize this is the end of the connection. "I hope to see you again someday," I blurt.

"Yes, dear. I do, too," she politely replies, the likeliness of that happening not lost on either of us.

She likes me. I'm so touched by her call, I could burst into tears the moment we hang up. Instead I start to laugh as I think of the day I met her seven-year-old granddaughter—B.H.'s niece. The second she had me to herself in Dolores' living room, little Krista, a precocious wisp of half-Maori blood, began her interrogation. "How old are you?" she asked, nuzzling against my chair. "How many children do you have?" she nonchalantly queried, fondling my dangling earrings. And the last of the questions obviously culled from adult conversation: "Why did you wear a black dress to your wedding?"

186

Whatever their initial reservations, his family embraced me in no time, and Dolores even threw a party at the farm in our honor. "I love the way you talk," one of his teenage cousins told me. "You sound like the Sopranos."

He's here in Vegas. How naïve of me to think he'd be safely tucked away up in Utah.

That ugly emotional scab is ripe for picking again, so I pull out the photo album holding the pictures of our trip to New Zealand. There's one he took of me hamming it up on the black sand of Kawhia, a resort town on the north island's west coast. My outstretched arms present the seaside backdrop like a toothy showcase model on *The Price is Right*, my giddy expression proclaiming, "Look! It's Christmas Eve and I'm at the beach!" I'd never been to the ocean during the winter months, and there I was frolicking on the shore in New Zealand, of all places. I'd come a long way.

Funny. I'd forgotten that I left a wash in the machine before we left Dolores' house that morning and while we were gone, she did us a favor and hung our laundry—everything—out back to dry. How mortified I was when we pulled into the driveway to find my collection of thongs neatly affixed to the clothes line. Thank God it was the new stuff I'd bought for the trip and not period underwear. Whatever went through her mind as she pierced the clothespins into the tiny bits of Lycra and lace, I pray is long forgotten.

I run my finger over a picture of him sitting in his mother's yard on Christmas Day. His hair is long and he looks younger than I remember; the outline of a pack of Marlboros bulges through his T-shirt pocket. Blue eyes squint down a beer bottle into the camera, defiantly announcing, "I'm on my way and there's nothing you can do about it." How true. He and his brothers went on the piss that night at the picnic table; I bonded with Dolores and his two sisters inside at the dining room table. We had great fun exchanging celebrity gossip rags; they devoured the *Us* and *People* magazines I brought from the States and I was equally enthused by their *Stella* magazine and the Australian version of *Cosmopolitan*.

They told me that the soap operas are about five years behind in New Zealand, which prompted an audible gasp and a promise to tape some episodes of *Days of Our Lives* for them.

"I'm so happy to be here with you," I told them. "I love my sisters back home, and I'm thrilled to have two more."

"We're happy to meet *you*. We didn't know what to expect," one admitted.

"Yeah, we thought you'd be a drinker, too," the other one said as she opened our second bottle of wine.

When I got back home I prepared a care package of videos, magazines, and L.L. Bean catalogs, which I mailed off with the altruism of a nun sending provisions to a third-world country. I can't bear to think I will never see them again.

He's here in Vegas. I get online to map out the address Dolores gave me. It's on Harmon, west of the Hard Rock. Jesus. The end of the semester—when shit is sure to hit the fan—and he's living in the shadow of the Las Vegas Strip, the epicenter of temptation. Perfect time and place for someone on a path of self-destruction.

§ § §

I pull into the parking lot of my divorce support group meeting, fifteen minutes early. Mona and I didn't have our usual Tuesday night dinner; she signed up with a nanny service and has a babysitting job at a casino on the Strip tonight. That's another thing she's tried to talk me into—babysitting. She says it's a great way to make a few bucks, but I told her don't push it, she's already roped me into subbing.

Though I miss getting together with her, I'm happy to have some alone time with Chuck, the facilitator. As it turns out, I'm the first one here. Chuck's already arranged the room and sits at the arc of a fifteen-chair horseshoe, in anticipation of this week's gathering of the souls in various states of anguish. Personally, I don't know how he can stand to listen to us week after week. The man's a saint.

I get right at it. "Hey, Chuck, you've been in town forever. What's that area like over on Harmon between the Strip and the Hard Rock?"

"It's bad," he tells me. "Drug dealers, prostitutes. A lot of crime. Why do you ask?"

"My ex has a place there."

"That's not good." I'm not used to seeing Chuck so serious, despite the discouraging nature of our group. "I'd be afraid if he's drinking, someone could roll him. Really." His concern spooks me.

I contemplate his words and smile weakly at the others as they start to file in. Tonight there are only about ten of us—the regulars. As per meeting protocol, Chuck asks us to assess our emotional barometer on a scale of one to ten, and when it's my turn, I report I'm a two. My response is met with questioning faces. "Yeah," I confirm, with a nod, "I'm a two."

I understand their surprise. Usually I'm at least a seven or eight; usually I'm the one offering encouragement to the others, pulling insights from my arsenal of spiritual coping mechanisms. I've been a sort of role model, the poster girl for making lemonade, especially to the new people. I proudly tell them how far I've come, how within six months of crash-landing in Las Vegas, I was able to pull myself together enough to try stand-up comedy, something I would never have tried if I were still married. But this is a different Linda sitting with them in the circle tonight.

To satisfy the inquiring minds that want to know, Chuck calls on me first to share. About three sentences into my woeful discourse,

Sanjay, the retired physician who came to see me perform at Boomers, interrupts.

"Your problem is, you don't love yourself," he states with one hundred percent certainty.

His words slap me into the moment.

"I don't love myself?" Reflexively, my right hand presses to my chest. I opt for levity while I process his words. "I'm the center of my own freakin' universe. Who could possibly be more self-absorbed than me?"

He remains steadfast. "You don't love yourself."

I try to stay calm, but self-defending words are never delivered with true serenity. "Do you know how hard I work on myself?" I ask him. "I spend half my freakin' life exercising, doing yoga, meditating… I have a whole library of self-improvement books, that I've actually read. With a highlighter. I don't know how I could possibly love myself more." God damn that *Absolutely No Swearing* sign.

"You worry too much about your ex-husband. If you loved yourself, you would go on with your life. You have to let him go." Sanjay is so sure of his truth, I want to kick his fucking ass. I look to my friend Leticia for support. I wish Mona were here.

"Let go and let God," he adds.

"You know," I start, my tone taking on what my kids used to call my "snotty voice," "I've heard this before. 'Go on with your life, let him go.' Sanjay, of all people, you should know that addiction is a disease, a disease of the brain. If he had cancer, do you think I'd be like, 'Too bad, that's your problem?'" I've thought about this a lot. Wouldn't Wendy go to the end of the earth to save Bob? "If one of my kids struggled with addiction, would I give up on him? No, I would leave no stone unturned. So why is it okay to give up on a spouse? I'm the only person in this hemisphere who loves him; he has no one else." Fuck! Anger through tears is my least favorite emotion.

I can tell Sanjay feels bad for upsetting me, yet he keeps on. "I want to say one more thing. That man you were with when you did your comedy, he was very drunk."

Oh, Christ. I shake my head, my eyes rolling back to my cerebellum. "That's my friend Chief. I've know him, like, twenty years."

"I would hate to see you get involved with him, that's all."

Jesus, what does he think, I'm one of those pathetic Burning Bed trailer park women who get the shit beat out of them and then wail, "But I love him!" And then when they finally do escape the abuse, they pick another loser and relive the same drama, but with a different player—is that how he thinks of me? Jesus Christ.

I blink deliberately and look at Chuck. "Next."

§ § §

I want to talk to him. Well, no—I really want to see him. I want to see how he looks; I want to make sure he's okay. After an email and three messages on his voicemail, he finally calls.

"Thanks for getting back to me," I say, as if he's a prospective employer responding to my resume. "I've been thinking of you. How are you doing?"

"I'm fine. Yeah. Glad the semester is over." *Se-may-stah.*

"You must be happy."

He pauses a few seconds. "Yeah, I got my grading done."

What the hell is he doing? Oh. "Are you in a bar?" I ask.

"Yeah." Of course he is. I hear him exhale away from the phone, which means he's smoking, too. He seems sober, though.

"How are you doing?"

"I'm okay."

"I've been wondering how your appointment with the cardiolo-

191

gist went."

Nothing. "Are you there?" Jesus Christ, can you grant me one goddamn morsel of attention?

"Yeah. Sorry, I was watching something on TV. Hey, I won a couple of big pots playing poker last night."

"Oh, really? Where are you? In Vegas?" Duh.

"Yeah, I took a place near the Hard Rock. The neighborhood's a bit dodgy, but I can walk to the Strip. Hey, I saw Ben Affleck in the race and sports book in the Bellagio a few nights ago. He seems like a nice guy, eh." The television must no longer be holding his attention. "Yeah, I've been doing really well. I put fifty dollars across the board on a horse that went off at thirty-eight to one. It came in, eh."

Like I give a crap. "That's good." Must be nice to have money to piss away gambling. "I'm leaving for Albany the day after tomorrow. Do you think we can get together before then, since you're here in town? It would be nice to see you."

Nothing.

"No. That probably wouldn't be a good idea."

I knew it. There's no use pressing, in fact, there's no reason to continue this conversation at all. There's nothing left of him, the demons are running the show. I try to think of the last time he asked me a question.

"Okay, then. Well, you're still in my heart. Take care of yourself. And I really would like to see you."

Nothing. "Yeah." And that's it.

*You're still in my heart...*Jesus, which one of us is more fucked up? Why the hell can't I let go? What exactly is there to hold on to?

I look out my kitchen window to the million lights of the valley and the Strip in the distance. He's out there somewhere. God, keep him safe.

§ § §

Church is not doing it for me anymore. The old guy means well, but he always seems to be scolding us, and I'm simply too fragile to endure his disapproving paternal nature. I liked the ladies' psychic church, but there's no way to gracefully duck out before they start in with the singing and hand-holding and throughout the sermon I find myself immersed in germ-phobic angst when I should be gaining enlightenment.

So tonight I'm attending a lecture by this man named Bijan. I heard him speak in Albany several years ago; I guess you'd call him a spiritual teacher. He's from Iran, and he's a former Mr. Universe. I remember him telling us how he would will himself a good parking spot outside the gym and then go in and run eight miles on the treadmill. I bought his book, *Effortless Prosperity*, and started doing the thirty-day program again last summer when I randomly pulled it from my bookshelf. I'm all for anything effortless, though quite frankly, the prosperity part has yet to kick in. At any rate, his principles make sense to me. Bijan says to make peace your only goal, and that the ego is the barrier to happiness. Fuck it—at this point I'll try anything that doesn't involve shaving my head and donning an orange robe.

In his book Bijan mentions he lives in Las Vegas, and I've been wondering if he's still here. Then last week I met a woman at one of those dreadful networking mixers where everyone's super-nice to you until they find out you're not in the market to buy real estate. How many mortgage originators can there possibly be? Anyway, her name is Maria and she told me Bijan gives free lectures every Friday night at the Course in Miracles church on West Charleston. She assured me there's no kum-bay-ah-ing at the end, so here I am.

Like so many churches in Las Vegas, the sanctuary is a rented storefront in a strip mall. About forty folding chairs face a small platform adorned with fresh flowers on either side. Behind the cushioned barstool positioned in the center of the platform is a sign that says, "God is Love." Framed passages from the Course hang from the walls—no scary images of Jesus holding sheep. I take a seat on the end of the back row and move my chair a few inches to the side in case someone sits next to me and has the nerve to start coughing or breathing in my direction.

Aside from a handful of older folks, these people look younger than those in the other churches I've sampled. "Religion comes with age," my friend Dick used to say. *Dick.* People don't call their kids Dick anymore. Just as well, especially when you get into the father/son "Big Dick/Little Dick" monikers. Kids have enough to screw them up these days.

Most everyone here seems to know each other and I watch them exchange warm embraces. The vibe is casual; many people are in jeans and the woman in the row in front of me is wearing army fatigues. She has a cute pixie haircut, dyed almost a magenta color. I bet she does yoga. The man she's with has thick salt and pepper hair and one of those affable faces that makes me think he's never had a pissed off moment in his life. He drapes his arm around Pixie Girl's shoulder and every so often gives her a loving glance and a squeeze. They seem cool, like I could be friends with them. Except they're obviously in love, which is enough to make me puke.

Bijan walks in and takes his place in the chair up front. His ageless muscle-man physique and shiny bald head form a striking presence that radiates throughout the room. I notice he sits with impeccable posture, and wonder if people approach him in the store, too, and ask for directions to the dressing rooms.

"Welcome, everybody," he says, flashing gleaming white teeth. "How is everyone doing tonight?" Bijan scans the crowd, his gaze directed slightly above the tops of our heads. "You know I can see your energy," he teases, "so you'd better tell the truth." Some of us chuckle.

"Before we get started, does anyone have a miracle to share?" he asks. A few people raise their hands and one by one they relate incidents involving unexpected good luck or episodes of amazing synchronicity. We all clap supportively after each person's story. I like the interactivity.

"Tonight I want to talk about judgment," Bijan says, in a heavy Middle Eastern accent. Judgment—I hope he hasn't been reading my mind. I've already decided that the lady in the front row is way too fat to tuck in her shirt, the man two chairs away really needs to trim that disgusting nose hair, and the woman across the aisle is about two weeks overdue for a root job. Bijan's eyes darken with intensity as he speaks about judgment being the work of the ego, yet overall the mood is light. Now and then he smiles broadly—not the over-friendly church lady smile or the desperate "Let me sell you a mortgage" smile—no, Bijan smiles as though he's suppressing a hilarious private joke that keeps popping back into his head.

He encourages questions. Pixie Girl asks if it's okay to be judgmental if it's in a positive way. That's something I want to know, too, because I was just thinking that Bijan's wife has the most incredible tits and I'll bet my last dime they're real. But no, he says we're not supposed to judge at all, good or bad.

"Any other questions?" he asks.

I raise my hand like a fifth grader who may or may not know the correct answer. "I have a question," I begin, though at this point I'm not sure it's fully formulated. "I know I've been judging my husband. My ex-husband, I mean." Shit. What am I saying? Fuck it, I'll let it rip. "He has problems with addiction. I'm worried about his health, I'm worried about his safety, and everyone tells me, 'You have to let go, you have to move on,' and I find myself judging them for saying that. I mean, they're really pissing me off." I don't know where I'm going with this; words continue to tumble. "And then I start judging myself because maybe they're right and I'm being stupid and maybe I should go on with my life. But I love him, and I didn't marry him to let him go." I shake my head. "Sorry. I don't know what my question is."

Bijan shrugs his shoulders as if it's a no-brainer. "You don't have to let him go." His eyes cast clear to the back of my skull. "You don't have to let him go," he repeats. "Just get out of his way."

He now addresses the room as a whole. "Let me explain. People are either going up, going down, or they're hovering where they are because they can't decide where they want to go. When people are on their way up, you want to support them to help their energy rise, to help boost them to where they need to be." Bijan motions with his hands to demonstrate. "But people on the way down must reach the bottom before they can go back up, and so you have to get out of their way." He pauses to nod in my direction. "Your husband can't go back up until he experiences the lessons he needs to learn at the bottom. If you get in his way, you prevent him from learning those lessons, and then it will take longer for him to head back up. Do you understand?"

I nod. "But wait, what if his bottom is really bad? What if..."

Bijan raises an index finger. "For some people the bottom is death," he says, his tone so matter-of-fact. "They come back to learn their lessons in the next life."

My nostrils flare to keep the tears from streaming. I am so fucking sick of crying and the kind support emanating from Bijan and some of the other people in the room fuels the emotions and actually makes me feel worse. Pixie Girl's eyes tell me she understands.

"You have no control over the path your husband has chosen," he continues. "So allow him his path, and honor it without judgment. Trust God to take care of him. Send him love and light. You don't have to let him go, but get out of his way."

Get out of his way. I can do that.

§§§

Why is it that I can hear something a million times and then like magic it finally sinks in? He's wanted me out of his way all along; even Lola could see that was the meaning behind *The Guide to Picking Up Girls.*

Let go and let God. I resented hearing those words from Sanjay, but that's essentially what Bijan said as well. I have to wonder, how could I have resisted the idea in the first place? Do I really think I can do a better job with him than God?

Surrendering something to God frees up brain space, not unlike a troublesome work project that you're suddenly able to pass off to a colleague. When you've truly surrendered, you feel a sense of relief, not loss; the only thing you lose is a sense of control you never had in the first place.

I can surrender him. Like poor Mr. Hiscock buried in the cemetery Bob used to mow on Long Island, he's in God's hands.

PART III

1.

During wintertime in Albany, the gray sky blends into the gray snow. Sometimes the gloom can last so long you have to remind yourself there is brightness on the other side of the clouds. I've been here for three days now, and boy, do I miss the warmth and sunshine. But it's good to be with my family, especially my kids and Connor.

Christopher seems taller to me, though at almost twenty-six, I'm sure he's stopped growing. I'd say he's at least six-four—long and lanky and usually dressed in Johnny Cash black. He's a gentle soul who says maybe twenty words during the course of a day, mostly monosyllabic, so having a conversation with Christopher is kind of like talking to Lurch. When he does have something to say, you can bet everyone listens, and when he really opens up, it's a treat; Christopher is the funniest person I know. He expresses himself beautifully through his art and his music, and people who know him are surprised to find he's quite the performer. He's the songwriter, the band's front man, and with the Dylan-esque metal harmonica holder wrapped around his neck, Christopher's learned to work the crowd despite his passive nature.

Maybe he's so quiet because he never got a word in edgewise once his younger sister made the scene. My mother used to say

Courtney was vaccinated by a Victrola needle; she seemed to have a full vocabulary at seven weeks. Like Christopher, Courtney's into art and music. If she had her way, this neo-hippie would follow the remaining members of the Grateful Dead around the country, selling her artwork and hemp jewelry.

Courtney looks more beautiful every time I see her. Over six feet tall in heels, she could pass for one of the models serving cocktails at the Palms. If anyone should be thankful for the gift of pulchritude, it's Courtney. When you come out with gems like, "Oh my God, did you know 'Saturday' has a 'u' in it?" it's good to have something to fall back on. She can laugh at herself, though. What a doll.

Connor is a precious child who, I like to think, resembles my kindergarten picture, except he has Courtney's freckles and porcelain-white skin. Neither of them could get a suntan if they lived at the equator. After Connor was born I remember Courtney saying, "I hope he turns out to be a sweet boy like Christopher." I was thrilled that she held her brother in such high esteem. Her wish came true; Connor has an adorable disposition. Now if I can only train him not to screech, *"Graaaan-neeey*, can you buy some baloney?"* while Granny is trying to flirt with the cute young deli guy.

Tonight the whole gang is at my mother's—there's Mom, the five of us kids, my sisters' husbands, all nine grandchildren, and Connor, the only great-grandchild, though he's actually older than my two youngest nephews. It's a freakin' madhouse, and this is only Christmas Eve. Tomorrow there's Christmas dinner, and then the next day Courtney's having a shindig at her place for Connor's fifth birthday, the real blessed event, if you ask me. Three consecutive days of Haber family bonding—that's a lot of noise.

It's okay, though. We have fun together, standing around the kitchen. We're "kitchen people." The adults, and I use that term loosely, file in and out to check the conversation at the moment or maybe to get another beer while the little kids raise hell, essentially unsupervised, in the living room. Everybody's talking at once, each person trying to be the predominant voice. Have they always been this loud, or have I just gotten used to the tranquility of living alone?

Fortunately, the Irish blood from my mother's side is diluted enough so it's not like we're pressing our thumbs into each other's Adam's apples at the end of the night; no one's hurling the Christmas tree, angel-first, into a snow bank. No, we all get along, and we're a young crowd, too; there's no ancient great-aunt to periodically check on or worry about pissing the couch. My mother's been the oldest person in the family since Granny died ten years ago, and she's not even seventy yet. And Mom's very hip.

"You know, I like that Pink Floyd," she says, commenting on the CD someone has deemed an appropriate choice to play on Christmas Eve. "If he ever comes to Albany, I would definitely go to see him in concert." We all exchange the look that says, "Let's let her run with this; it's gonna be good."

"Is he a gay man?" she asks, sipping her vin rose. "Not that it matters. He's an excellent musician." Yes, our mother is very hip.

My brother shakes his head. "You know what makes me nervous?" He points to Mom's feet. "Her heels are getting wider."

"What the hell does that mean, Steven? Are you saying these are old lady shoes? They're Nine West, for Christsake!" Mom yells above the cacophonous laughter.

My kids love it when we get their granny going.

"All I know is I'm not wiping her ass when she gets old," my sister Lori tells us, continuing to talk about our mother in the third person though she's standing right there.

"Gee, I thought I'd be far away in New Zealand, sending money for the home health aide," I say. There's a blip of silence, but it passes in no time. "And now she's moving to my side of the Mississippi.

Great…" I throw my head back as far as I can without losing my balance.

"Oh, piss on you all! Jim will take care of me," Mom says, too happy to feign indignation.

"Lucky Jim!" the choir responds.

Mom sold her house a few weeks ago and shortly after the first of the year will be moving out to Idaho to live with her boyfriend. She and Jim met at a singles dance about ten years ago after she and my father split up. Jim's originally from out West and thinks Boise will be a good place for them to settle for a while. Mom's up for the adventure—she has to make up for a lot of lost time. Let's hope Jim doesn't turn out to be an alcoholic who leaves Mom stuck in the middle of Potatoland. On my side of the Mississippi.

No, Jim's great, and we all like him a hell of a lot more than some of the other men she's paraded before us. There was Harold, the creepy guy missing a front tooth, and Arthur, who was nice enough, but he had to be 110, maybe 120 years old. Then there was Howie. Hmmm…We haven't pulled out the Howie story in a while. The kids will enjoy this.

I throw the first pitch. "Hey, you guys, remember Howie?"

Steven's right on it. "You mean the skinny Jewish guy whose questions always came in pairs?" He puts on his best Jackie Mason. *"Where are you going? You going out?"*

"Oh, he drove me nuts," Mom says. "He thought he was so funny, and he'd say, 'What's the matter? You don't think I'm funny?' and I told him, 'Look, I was married to the funniest man on earth, so don't even try.'"

"Remember when you broke up with him? Remember what he did?" I ask, my questions prompting beer to blow out of my sister Lisa's nose. My youngest sister, Stacie, nearly drops the two-month-old baby in her arms.

"What? What did he do, Granny?" Courtney begs to know. "Tell us!"

"He didn't take it too well, Court," I say, and then hand the stage over to Mom.

"Well, Courtney, the morning after I broke up with him," she starts, in a *Once upon a time voice*, "my boss pulled me into her office and said, 'Diane, I got a call from Howie Fischer last night' and I thought oh, Jesus Christ. Well, Howie told her everything I'd ever said about her." She shakes her head. "It wasn't good."

"Granny! Shut *up*! What did you do?" I knew Courtney would be digging this.

"What could I do? I said, 'Yes, I did call you a bitch.'"

Courtney crosses her legs to keep from peeing. We're all losing it. Even Christopher is smiling.

"Well she was," Mom says, and then adds the moral of the story. "You can't lie, honey. It's not right."

This is our last Christmas in the kitchen on Lincoln Avenue. There's no sense of nostalgia; the neighborhood's been declining for years. The one- and two-family clapboard houses, where four same-sex kids would cram into tiny bedrooms with two sets of bunk beds, are no longer owner-occupied. Absentee landlords now rent their properties to anyone who can tolerate the lack of off-street parking and living in houses so close together that in the summer, you can hear your neighbors' silverware clink on their plates. Today drug deals transpire on the narrow red brick road where we used to play kickball until the streetlights came on. We're glad Mom's getting out.

Times change. People change, too, though you can't change anyone and you certainly can't tell anyone what to do. You can't tell them to become a Democrat, love Jesus, or stop drinking, regardless of the benefits they'd enjoy if only they'd follow your sage advice.

No, you can't tell anyone anything, and you can't change anyone. But people do change.

My mother spent half my childhood and most of my teen years sacked out on the couch, doped up on nerve pills that were supposed to help her agoraphobia. Though she'd venture out with my father to fulfill important parental obligations such as teacher conferences, school award ceremonies, and ballet recitals, other than that, she never seemed to leave the house, and certainly never alone.

I remember hanging out in my best friend's bedroom one afternoon, watching her inspect a blouse her mother had picked up for her. As she twisted her eyebrows in disapproval, all I could think was, Wow, your mother went to the store all by herself? And she laid a blouse on your bed for you to find when you got home from school? How can you not like it? The only thing I'd ever found laid out after school was my mother's body under the afghan.

Things changed when Mom started to come back to life in her mid-forties, my age now. I don't know what specifically led to it, but somehow, like me, she ended up in a support group, except hers was filled with a bunch of What About Bobs. I think most of them had agoraphobia, but some had more specific fears, like the woman who was so afraid of birds she made her daughter cut all the bird pictures out of magazines so she wouldn't have to look at them. That actually doesn't seem too nutty to me; I freaked out when I saw one flying inside the grocery store last week. I would have abandoned my shopping basket, but it was almost *Guiding Light* time and I really needed my ice cream.

On occasion, Mom's group went on field trips to practice walking through the mall, paying a cashier, and riding elevators and escalators—mundane activities that could have sent any of them into a panic. Eventually Mom got to the point where one morning, a few weeks after Christopher was born, she took a city bus some sixteen

206

blocks to our apartment. All by herself.

"I made it!" she cried, standing at my door, flush with jubilation. She then recounted every detail of her journey like she was Neil Armstrong returning home after splashdown.

More victories followed. Soon after, she enrolled in a night class at Albany High, which led to a part-time job as a bookkeeper at a non-profit agency several blocks up the street, her first job in almost three decades, and home of the infamous bitch boss. One of her friends taught her how to drive, and in a couple of years she was driving herself to work in a brand new 1986 Dodge Omni.

Realizing that twenty years of sitting through *Jeopardy* was no substitute for a formal education, Mom enrolled in classes at one of the community colleges and at age fifty-eight, was awarded an associate's degree in accounting. Three years ago, at sixty-six, she took her first business trip—to midtown Manhattan of all places—as the personal bookkeeper for a former New York State governor. The thought of my mother, who was once unable to step off the front porch, walking through Times Square makes me believe with all my heart that anything is possible.

I look around the kitchen and am overcome with the joy of the present moment. Life is good. My mother's healthy and happy, and soon she'll be off to Idaho. *Idaho!* My kids and siblings and nieces and nephews are all doing well. I take in their presence with every breath, trying to burn their images into my brain, wishing I could bottle the roar of their laughter because in no time I'll be back in Vegas, missing them.

And in the perfection of this present moment, I think of B.H. and I can't help but wonder—what must it be like to spend Christmas Eve alone in a casino?

§ § §

My first ex-husband and I sit on Courtney's couch in the glow of the Christmas tree lights, our sleeping grandson's body draped across my lap.

"He's out cold," Chris says, rubbing the little shin that peeks out between Connor's Sponge Bob pajamas and slippers.

I nod. "Another big day. Gets pretty exhausting opening a million birthday presents the day after you open a million Christmas presents."

"I should move him to his bed."

"No, not yet," I tell him. "I'm not ready to give him up."

Neil Young's *Harvest Moon* and the Indian bedspreads on the walls trigger an enjoyable déjà vu. Courtney's apartment feels like the places we used to have. Same music, same old furniture from dead relatives—Nana's telephone stand, Daddy's couch and coffee table, the rattan chairs from Granny's patio. Courtney has my bohemian taste in decorative accessories and shares my philosophy that one can't have too many candles. Even the Christmas tree looks familiar, since Courtney inherited the family decorations when I moved out West. Her "Baby's First Christmas 1979" ornament hangs directly under a fragile green bulb that came from Granny's first Christmas tree in 1912. Deliberate placement, I bet. Courtney loved her great-grandmother.

"I see the angels at the top of the tree again this year," I comment, referring to a picture of the band U2 pasted onto a yellow cardboard star. It's held the special place atop Blackwell family Christmas trees for about fifteen years.

"I made that," my son says, rising from a dining room chair behind the couch.

"Gee, honey, I didn't know you were back there." I look at his father. "Remember when he'd stand on the vacuum cleaner and sing into the handle, pretending he was Bono?"

The two of us watch Christopher's lanky frame bend over the stereo to change the CD. I hug our slumbering little one and wonder if Chris, too, feels sadness over the alarming rate time seems to pass.

I don't recognize Christopher's music selection. "This is nice. Who is it?"

"Will Oldham."

"Nice." Chris and I turned the kids on to our music, and now they're introducing us to a new generation of artists. We sit listening.

"So you're divorced again," my former husband says.

I can't resist the opportunity to tease. "Yeah—why? You interested?"

Courtney comes in from the kitchen, finally done cleaning the mess from the birthday party.

"Mom and Dad are getting back together," Christopher announces.

The drama queen kneels in front of the tree, closes her eyes, and presses her hands together. "My prayers have been answered! It's a Christmas miracle!"

Chris and I exchange looks. We've stayed more than pleasant to each other in the ten years since we split up, and not just for the sake of the kids. I like Chris. He's a good man and a loving father, which makes it easier for me to live away from the kids on the other side of the country. Though we'll never get back together, no doubt he'll go down in history as my most genial ex. And most normal. Least insane.

Courtney takes a seat on the floor at my feet and rubs that same patch of Connor's exposed skin. "He's mad cute, huh, Mom? Sometimes I can't stop looking at him."

I stroke his hair. "He sure is beautiful, Court."

She rests her head on my leg. "Did you used to look at me like that when I was little?"

"Of course, sweetie," I say, now stroking her hair. "I still look at you that way. Christopher, too. You'll always be my babies, no matter how old you are."

She considers my words. "I never thought of that." And for the first time, I realize that my mother will always look at me that same way, too, no matter how old I get.

Courtney sighs. "I wish I didn't have to go to work tomorrow." Here comes the scowl. "I'm sorry, Mom, but I was not put on this earth to work in a fucking cubicle."

I pretend to ignore Chris clearing his throat and address our daughter. "No, you weren't, honey. And don't say the f-word. It sounds trashy."

§ § §

With three straight days of family activities behind me, I now have a chance to connect with my friends. Every time I go back to Albany, a bunch of us get together for happy hour at the Washington Tavern, the "WT," a neighborhood Irish bar frequented by old-time Albanians until the students take over later in the evening. I arrive first and claim my favorite barstool near the front window.

"Well, look who's here!" Mark the bartender leans over a row of drying glasses to give me a kiss on the cheek. I've known Mark a long time; his brother bought the house across from ours on Lincoln Avenue back when I was in high school.

"Where are you these days? Did I hear you're living in Utah?"

"No, I was in Utah, but I've been in Vegas for six months now."

"That's right. Your sister Lori told me you're doing stand-up comedy?" That's a question, not a statement.

"Just a couple of times. So far."

"Yeah, I couldn't believe that," he says, handing me a Guinness.

I let out a little laugh. Lori told me that every single person who hears I'm doing stand-up responds with, "Really? I didn't know Linda was funny."

How different it is to be here, getting served by a bartender who actually knows me in a tavern that's close to a hundred years old. Nothing's old in Vegas, especially where I live in Henderson. I drive around Albany and think, "Wow, this place is already built." No cranes gracing the skyline, no construction equipment planted amid skeletons of housing developments and strip malls. Albany is an old city, and though the downtown area has some beautiful structures, rich with history and architectural design, most of the rest of the city strikes me as dingy and depressing.

Folks stopping for a pint after work file in, as do my friends. Each one greets me with a big hug. "You look great!" I hear, to my delight.

"Oh, stop!" I protest, in the most shamelessly phony way. "All I've done lately is eat and drink. I bet I've gained five pounds, six maybe." They roll their eyes. "My gut's, like, hanging over my belt. I should be wearing a burka."

Chuckie Bell, one of the boys I grew up with on Lincoln Avenue, puts his arm around me. "Linda, I'm glad to see you haven't changed a bit."

"That's not true, Chuck," I say, flaunting my Vegas cleavage in the middle of sweater season. "You can't tease me about being on the Itty Bitty Titty Committee anymore."

"So, Lin, do you miss Albany?" Patty, my roommate from college asks.

Hell, no! is my knee-jerk reaction, but I respond carefully; these people still live here. "I miss my family and friends. But the city itself…" *Be kind.* "You know, there's no Lark Street in Vegas," I say, referring to an area bordering downtown. I do miss seeing restored brownstones, trendy bars and funky restaurants, hip little shops displaying Birkenstocks and alpaca sweaters in their windows. "There's no place in Vegas to park the car and walk around," I continue. "And there's no place like Albany in the summertime."

That's true. From Memorial Day until early fall, Albany's cultural calendar is peppered with all kinds of free events—theatre in the park, street fairs, and lots of music festivals. "The music scene is much better in Albany," I tell them. "I did find a zydeco band that plays in one of the casinos, and the biker bars have good blues bands." I sip the last of my beer. "But mainly we get the big headliners in the arenas and the 'past-peak' entertainers in the showrooms, which I call 'the career hospice.'" I'm corny tonight. "But the more eclectic artists don't seem to come through. I wouldn't know where to find a bluegrass band or folk music." Another Guinness magically appears in front of me.

"Hey, I heard you're a stand-up comedian now," my friend Dick says. *Dick.*

"No, Dickie, I've done a couple of open mics, that's it."

"On the Strip?"

How preciously naive. "Um, not exactly," I reply. My friends have many wide-eyed questions about life in Las Vegas, and I'm thankful they're more curious about my comedy than my marital status. The fact I'm doing stand-up is probably a lot more surprising.

Christopher and Courtney are here, chatting it up with everyone. Out of the corner of my ear I hear someone asking Christopher how tall he is now and another commenting on Courtney's good looks. These friends have known my kids since before they were born. It's wonderful to be with people who helped mold my life's permanent record, people who know my siblings, who remember my mother when she slept the day away, who laughed at the stories during my father's eulogy.

"Do you think you'll ever move back?" Patty asks.

I don't have to think long before answering. "No, I don't." She looks a bit disappointed, so I add, "Well, never say never, but I don't see it happening anytime soon."

That's because the sense of history I appreciate and draw comfort from is precisely what I'm happy to be away from. No one out West knows me as Linda Haber, the skinny little cheerleader from Lincoln Avenue. Sometimes you have to leave the place where you grew up so you can grow into the person you were meant to be. Then you'll be funny enough to do stand-up comedy, and it won't even matter if you're performing in front of a shower curtain in the back room of a dive bar.

§ § §

My flight gets into Vegas around 10:00 tonight, New Year's Eve. Whatever. It's not like I have any exciting plans. Happy to have a window seat, I settle in and pull the essentials from my carry-on— my *People* and *US* magazines, *USA Today*, reading glasses, retractable pencil, and Altoids—and arrange them in the pocket of the seat in front of me. A slender college girl with long blond hair smiles at me as she takes the seat on the aisle. I smile back over the top of my glasses, pencil in hand, newspaper neatly folded to the crossword and think, how cool am I? I must look ancient to her.

I had a great time in Albany, but I'm itchy to get back. To what, I don't know. I guess I'll start subbing Monday, if they call me. Shit. I close my eyes and pray for the good health of every single teacher in the Clark County School District.

Having the middle seat remain empty would be too good to be true, and sure enough, it belongs to one of the last passengers to board, a well-dressed woman about ten years older than me. Her strawberry blond Dorothy Hamill hair falls to her face as she places an expensive looking briefcase under the seat in front of hers, and then springs back into place as she raises her head. I like her, she emits a warm energy. After she gets herself situated, I say, "Poor you, stuck the middle."

"Yeah, I hate the middle." Her thick New York accent belies her gentle looks. "I don't like the aisle, either. People bumpin' into you, and then you have to get up to let 'em pee every half hour."

"I know, that's so annoying." The basis for a good relationship, however fleeting, is not whether you share the same interests, but whether the same things piss you off.

"They should go before they get on the plane, right?" she asks.

"Absolutely. And don't worry, I already went." She reminds me of my friend Michael back in Cedar City, so delightfully opinionated.

"I'm just glad you're petite," I say, "being in the middle and all."

"It's funny you say that." She raises her index finger. "I travel a lot, for business. Now picture this. I'm at the window and another woman's on the aisle, and we're talkin', ya know?"

I nod.

"And I see this man, I swear he's like four hundred pounds, headin' down the aisle, and I say to her, 'Watch this big fat guy sit right between us.' And she says, 'Oh, he will. That big fat guy is my husband.'"

I cup my hands over my face and giggle into my palms. "Oh, my God! What did you do?"

"I thought I would *die*." She shakes a finger at me. "He literally could not fit into the seat. And you know what they did? They put him up in first class, can you believe that? For bein' a big fat guy, he gets first class."

Dorothy turns out to be the perfect middle seat stranger. Every now and then we share a sarcastic observation, but for the most part allow ourselves solitude. My celebrity rags keep my mind off whatever lies in front of me in the New Year.

"So did 2003 suck or what?" I ask at one point, out of nowhere.

She peers at me over her reading glasses. "Yes," she says. "Yes, it did."

§ § §

The line at the taxi stand snakes around three layers of ropes corralling New Year's Eve revelers eager to don their party hats. They annoy the hell out of me. I wish Mona could've picked me up, but she's celebrating tonight with her married friends. Poor Mona. The only thing worse than having no one to kiss at midnight is being surrounded by people who do. After about forty-five minutes, an attendant's whistle summons me to a cab. The driver is not happy about going all the way out to Henderson. Too bad—I'm not happy it'll cost me thirty bucks. We sit in silence while the meter rolls.

Aaaah, it's nice to be back in my apartment. I plop into the couch and turn on the TV to my friends at the Weather Channel. I'll unpack later. Maybe tomorrow.

My apartment looks so tidy, sparse even. Back in Albany, I noticed people's houses are loaded with all kinds of crap. Drawers full of Tupperware; countertops cluttered with small appliances; bookshelves, buffets, china closets, and curios—every horizontal surface—covered with knick-knacks they've accumulated over the years. Attics and basements and garages full of snow blowers, lawn mowers, garden hoses, gas grills—so much to take care of. I get overwhelmed thinking of it, though I used to have all that stuff, too. Not anymore—after three moves in two years, I'm down to the essentials, the things that truly bring me joy. Everything else got tossed.

It's liberating to lighten your load; your possessions can weigh on you. Sometimes I look around this place and think I could pack up and be out of here in about six hours. Not that I'm planning to move again, but it's nice to know I could if I wanted to. After being a settler for so many years, I consider myself an explorer now, and I know damn well I'd still be in Albany anchored with a jam-packed house if it weren't for Bastard Husband.

In his *Effortless Prosperity* book, Bijan says sometimes people come into your life as boats. Their sole purpose to take you from one place to another—geographically or spiritually—and once you're where you're supposed to be, they've fulfilled their mission and they move out of your life.

So I married a boat? I thought I married a life partner, someone to share adventures with till death do us part, not for a mere three-year period. Like many, I mourn the loss of what never will be more than the chaos that actually was.

My messages! I jump up from the couch. I couldn't check them in Albany, since I forgot the remote access code for this new voice-mail on my phone. What? I've been gone over a week and there are only two?

The first one's from Bob, my GE buddy. He can talk again! His voice sounds a little weakened, but it's our beloved Bob's voice. He's done with his treatments and as far as anyone can tell, the cancer's gone. Thank you, God, a million times!

The second message is from Debbie, the volunteer coordinator at the hospice...Lola died...the day after Christmas.

Dull pops in the distance signal the beginning of the New Year. I watch the fireworks shoot over the Strip as my brain begs to imagine where B.H. is right now. I refuse to pick that scab, though it's a safe bet he's not kissing anyone, either.

Lola's dead. Dammit.

2.

I hadn't expected to go up at Boomers tonight, but Marcus called this afternoon and said he didn't have enough comics in the lineup and could I do a quick set. So here I am, decked out in one of my sleazy Ross Dress-for-Less comedy blouses. This works out well—Cozy has me booked at some bar on Wednesday night, and it'll be good to get some stage time in beforehand.

Smelly Dick Boy is doing his Italian-Puerto Rican shtick right now, and then I'm up after a guy named Perry. I've seen Perry only once before; he delivers his act perched on a stool. He's a sit-down comic.

My neck is a mess of blotches, I'm sure. I wrote some affirmations to burn into my mind during my pre-performance meditation ritual. Hopefully they'll help my stage fright.

I connect with the light within and approach my performance with joy.

As I walk to the stage I empower myself with the confidence of the universe.

Whatever. What I really need to remember is my set, especially my new "Utah Jesus vs. Vegas Jesus" bit. The hospice material goes over well, but I'm not up for that tonight. I stopped in there after church this morning and the place bummed me out big-time. Imagine feeling depressed in a hospice?

It was tough going into Lola's old room because I miss her, of course, and to make it worse, there on the edge of her bed sat a young kid, about 20 years old, in his pajamas, laughing with his friends. I smiled as I dutifully replaced his plastic water pitcher with fresh ice chips, but the sadness of seeing a hospice patient my kids' age overcame me and I almost lost it on my way out of the room. Then in the hallway I ran into that old biddy Bernadette, the cleavage-hating chaplain. I grinned and sashayed past her like a runway model, just to piss her off, and she gave me the stink eye.

My friend Neil is here to see me perform tonight. Neil reminds me of the little Jewish guys I was friends with in junior high—long, thick black hair parted on the side, still waiting for the growth spurt everyone's been talking about. I met him at that stupid networking meeting I went to last fall. We winced in unison as a man rifled through a bowl of mixed nuts right after he coughed into his hand, and then the two of us talked for twenty minutes about how we'd rather starve than eat bar nuts left open to mass contamination. Neil and I meet for lunch now and then, having determined that the restaurant chain Baja Fresh meets our strict sanitation standards. He says his girlfriend teases him about his Howard Hughes tendencies, but if you ask me, she's a lucky woman; most men have no appreciation for germs. I'm glad Neil's here; he's good moral support.

Smelly Dick Boy's done with his set and Marcus brings Perry to the stage. Perry has a Beatle haircut, which normally is not exactly a turn-on, but together with the black rimmed glasses and Pink Floyd t-shirt, he looks cool as hell. I wonder how old he is. Definitely older than most of the other comics. I doubt he's forty, though. Shit. Probably too young for me, though I can go pretty young. "As long as they can drive at night," I used to say. No doubt I'll apply that same rule when I'm an old bat screening boyfriends in the assisted living home.

Perry's humor is intelligent, and unlike a lot of the comics here, he doesn't go for the tasteless, low-hanging fruit. He seems so relaxed, maybe because he's sitting. No, I bet he's just a really cool guy. I never see anyone who turns me on, but I am digging him, man. I bet he's a good kisser; he doesn't look like the slobber-all-over-you type. Omigod, what am I doing fantasizing about Perry? I should be mentally rehearsing my set! What the hell is wrong with me?

Perry winds up and I sit on the edge of my seat awaiting my turn. Again Marcus introduces me as "The Beautiful Linda Lou," God bless him. During my walk to the stage, I remember to empower myself with the confidence of the universe. I take the mic from Marcus and everything goes smoothly until the middle of my commentary on today's superior bra technology.

"Thanks to Victoria's Secret, anyone can have a great rack," I say, boosting my padded chest with my hands. "These are A cups in real life." *Ha, ha.* "Objects are much smaller than they appear." *Ha, ha, ha.* "Really, it's the Miracle bra you should…" No. That's not how it goes. "Fuck," I say, in a stage whisper. *Little ha-ha.* I throw up my hands as if I'm amazed this could possibly happen. "The line is, 'It's the *Wonderbra* you should wonder about.' I blew my joke!" *Polite laugh.* "Actually, I've blown a lot of"—quotation marks in the air— "jokes." *Big laugh.* I don't know where that came from, but that was a good save, Linda Lou.

I deliver the rest of my material only slightly ruffled, my judgmental out-of-body self forgiving me. Missteps are inevitable for those who brave the mighty risks of the stage; no one gets through comedy unscathed. I hand the microphone back to Marcus and people seem to clap with the same enthusiasm I've heard after my previous performances, so I guess it was no big deal. Like a good friend, Neil congratulates me when I get back to our table. "I like the new Jesus stuff," he says.

"Can you believe it? It's the old line I screwed up." I glance around, in search of Perry. *Perry.* Even his name is cool. Where is he? Maybe out at the bar. Or maybe he left. Shit.

Joe Lowers, the goofy middle-aged kid in his trademark bowling shirt, is again tonight's headliner. Everything that comes out of his mouth cracks me up, no matter how inane. I learn a lot from Joe. He's been performing on the road for years and I appreciate his willingness to share his expertise. One Sunday night he critiqued the other comics in my ear as we sat together in the back of the room. "This guy's talking to those girls up front and ignoring everyone else. You can't do that. Look at where he left the microphone. That's a barrier with the audience. Amateur. Always take the mic off the stand and move it behind you. First thing." When Joe offers advice, I hang on to his every word.

At the end of the show, I hug Neil good-bye and then linger with the other comics as they huddle around the sign-up booth waiting to get on Marcus' calendar for stage time. Danny Wilborn, a classically tall, dark and handsome guy in his early thirties, pulls me aside.

"I messed up," I acknowledge, before he can say it first.

"No, you didn't. People laughed." As gorgeous as Danny is, he'd be even better looking if he'd crack a smile now and then. I like his stuff; he's a funny comic, but man, is he serious. "You know why they laughed?" he asks.

"Not really."

Joe Lowers comes over. "You said 'fuck.'"

"That totally slipped out," I explain. "I try not to swear on stage. Off stage, I could make the Soparanos blush."

"You surprised your audience. That's good." Joe likes the mentor role.

Danny nods. "Nobody expects that out of you. You look so

sweet."

"I do?"

"Yeah," he says, his piercing black eyes devoid of emotion. "You're like a sweet…mom."

Okay, handsome, that's not the look I'm going for, but at least you said "mom" and not "granny."

"Really, dirty it up a little," Joe says. "We want to hear more about the jokes you've blown." He pushes his tongue in and out of his cheek.

I thank them and consider their words as I head for the door.

"Linda Lou!" someone calls. I turn around and it's—oh, my God—it's Perry. "You heading out?" he asks. "Can you stay and have a drink?"

"I'd love to!" Linda Haber, the bubbly cheerleader gushes. "But I have to get up early tomorrow. I…I have to be a substitute teacher." Did I say that with a straight face?

"Too bad." Jesus, he's even hotter up close. "Some other time? I think you're really funny."

"Oh, thanks. Yeah, definitely. I just don't want to, you know, go in hung over my first day." I giggle like an idiot. "But, after the first day, well, who the hell cares, right?"

Perry thinks I'm funny. What do people in Albany know?

§ § §

What is that fucking noise?

Oh, the alarm. It's been a while.

Howard Stern keeps me company as I shower, do my make-up, and put on the outfit I wore for my interview at the Hard Rock. That's a good choice—professional, but not farty. My hair is actually okay today, not that I have to look gorgeous for a bunch of seventh graders. Too bad it looks so crappy in this picture they're making me hang around my neck. Experimenting with highlights the day before they take the ID photo—not a good idea. I look much more attractive in my hospice volunteer badge. Maybe I'll switch and see if anyone notices.

The school is in a nice section of the Green Valley area of Henderson, just a short drive from my apartment. Do I park in the faculty lot, or am I a visitor? The answer's probably in the guest teacher handbook I left on the table at home. That reminds me—we're not supposed to call ourselves "substitutes," we're "guest teachers." Well, since I'm a guest, I pull into a space marked "Visitor."

"I'm here to sub for Evelyn Lansing's class," I tell the lady at the front desk in the dean's office.

"Yes, thank you for coming in," she says, with a glance to my crappy-headed ID. Her cheery tone tells me she's used to getting up early. "We're extremely short today. This is your room," she says, circling a number on a map she pulled out of an orange folder. "Building Four is opposite the library. In this envelope you'll find two keys—one to the classroom and the smaller one is for Mrs. Lansing's desk. Emergency procedures are right here." I gulp. *Please, God, no fire drills and, I beg of you, no school lockdowns.*

"And here's the bell schedule," she continues. "You have lunch period C." With that, she closes the folder. "Bring this back to me at the end of the day. And you're all set!"

They'll let anyone do this.

I find the lesson plan on Mrs. Lansing's desk, along with a note saying thank you and I should leave my name and phone number so next time she can call me directly instead of going through the automated system. That's nice.

Okay, so what do I have to do? The lesson plan says to go over the homework, but don't bother collecting it…remind the students that Friday is the last day to submit their projects for the science fair… and the remainder of the time have them watch the Bill Nye the Science Guy video. Wait, where is it? Oh, already in the VCR. Good. I fool with the clicker to make sure everything works. There's still fifteen minutes before all hell breaks loose.

Okay, I'm under control. I write "Good morning! Linda McNeil, Guest Teacher" on the whiteboard. Wait, I should probably change it to "Ms." McNeil, right? Why can't they just call me Linda? Or Linda Lou would be fine.

The first bell rings. I stand at the open door smiling like a Realtor, and as each student files past me, the clatter amplifies another notch. *"Yes! A sub!"* a voice in the mix says. I try to keep an eye on the developing free-for-all while I greet the kids still coming in and have a flash of panic when I realize I left my open pocketbook on the teacher's chair. The bell rings again and I close the door and get down to business. The decibel level is now comparable to a Sonic Youth show.

With arms folded over my chest, I position myself at the front of the room, trying to look stern, and realize I'm nothing but a forty-six-year-old woman playing school. The kids eventually quiet down to the point where I can be heard.

"Good morning, everyone! I'm Ms. McNeil. How you doing today?"

"Where's Mrs. Lansing?"

"Um, she's not here today," I answer brilliantly. "Now before we get started, as an introduction, I'm going to write three sentences about myself on the board. One of them is a lie. You have to guess which one." This has their attention. "But no talking while I write. In fact, no talking unless I call on you, okay?"

"She says 'tawk-ing.'"

"Miss McNeil! Miss McNeil! Are you from New York?"

I print "I am from New York City" on the whiteboard.

"Yes! I knew it!"

I turn around. "Wha'd I say? No talking unless I call on you."

"I told you! She says 'cawl.'"

The next sentence is "I am a grandmother," and then I write, "I do stand-up comedy." The kids shout their answers. "Hold on!" I try not to yell. "Shhh…"

Again with the folded arms and authoritarian yoga posture.

"Shhhh!!!"

"You guys! Shut up! This is fun!"

I'm glad they're digging this. "Okay, we're gonna take a vote. And you can vote only once." I point to the first sentence. "Raise your hand if you think I'm lying about being from New York City."

"You're from New Jersey."

"No, she's from Boston."

"Hmmm…Not too many of you think that's a lie." I write "6" next to sentence number one.

"Now, who thinks I'm lying about being a grandmother?" Thankfully, there's a sea of hands.

"You're too young!"

"Who said that?" I ask. A cute little thing tentatively raises her hand. "You're absolutely right," I tell her. "I do look much too young to be a grandmother, and you…are my favorite kid. No homework for you tonight." A few of them laugh. I write "13" next to the middle sentence.

"Last one. Who thinks I'm lying about doing stand-up comedy?"

"That one's the lie!"

"Yeah, she doesn't look funny."

I count sixteen hands. Or about that. The kids wait for me to come clean.

"Do you notice how quiet it is right now? Do you think you can be this quiet for the rest of the period?"

"Come on! Tell us!"

"Okay, the false statement is…" I milk the silence for as long as I can. "The first sentence. I am not from New York City."

A nerdy boy in a plaid shirt jumps out of his seat, fists raised above his head like a champion. "I told you! She's from New Jersey!"

"No, I'm not from New Jersey. I am from New York State, but not New York City. I'm from the capital of New York. Who knows what the capital of New York is?" Hey, look—I'm being educational!

A hand shoots up, but before I can call on him, somebody blurts *"Al-bany!"*

"That's right," I say, "but it's not 'Al-bany.' The correct pronunciation is 'Aw-benny.' There's a 'w' in it. Not many people know that." They like that I'm teasing them. This is kind of fun.

A boy with skater hair raises his hand. "So you really are a stand-up comic?" he asks in a low voice.

"Tell us a joke!"

"Yeah, tell us a joke!"

"Comics really don't tell jokes." Now I've taught them two things.

Skater Boy shakes his hair. "They do observational comedy," he coolly informs the class, then looks at me for validation of his statement. I nod. Skater Boy's hip.

"Come on, make us laugh!"

Though I'm sure they'd love to hear my ruminations on why women should never waste their money on implants, I motion with my hands to quiet down. "Let's go over the homework." For the next ten minutes, I read each problem, solicit answers, and then slyly consult the teacher's manual for verification, stopping a million freakin' times to tell them to keep it down.

During the video I sit at the big desk up front and browse through the orange folder. Lunch period C means I have four classes before lunch and two after—and *yes!*—my last class is a prep period. Because I'm a sub, I don't have to stay for that, which means my day ends at 1:20. Yippee! I'll stop for a vat of mocha almond fudge on my way home and I'll be all set for *Guiding Light* by two o'clock.

Seven more minutes. Bill Nye's enthusiasm is lost on me, and I decide I'm not much of a science person. Atoms, molecules, chemicals—I can't wrap my head around that stuff. If I can't see something, I'm not entirely convinced it exists. That's why I like art.

The bell rings as the video comes to an end—perfect timing. The kids stuff their books and papers in their backpacks and rush out.

"Tell us a joke next time!"

"Yeah, we want to hear some jokes."

Skater Boy approaches me. "Are you coming back tomorrow?"

"No, this is a one-day gig."

He nods. "Okay. I was just wondering."

Having survived the first fifty-three minutes, I'm ready to go home. Unfortunately, there's a fresh crop of kids rushing in.

Each class loves the three sentence game, and by third period, I no longer need to consult the answer key. Of *course*, the layer of earth found between the crust and the core is called "mantle"—*duh!*

Fourth period. Eighteen minutes till lunch and I've had quite enough of Bill Nye the Science Guy. My mind wanders. That creepy looking kid in the second row looks like he hasn't showered in two weeks. I think he actually does have cooties; clinically diagnosed, I bet. I like the good-looking kid with an English accent. Hmmm...I wonder what his father looks like.

Lunch period C comes not a moment too soon. I order a cheeseburger from the lunch lady at the window in the teachers' lounge and claim an empty table in the corner next to two real teachers discussing the challenges posed by "No Child Left Behind." How do they do this every freakin' day? And they make like, what? Thirty-five, forty thousand a year? God bless them. I secretly send them positive vibes through my open hand under the table, then pull a notebook out of my bag and try to come up with some funny blow job material for Boomers next week.

One more period to go. Despite my waning enthusiasm, I go through the motions of my three sentence game. What the hell— soon I'll be heading for *Guiding Light*. I am sooo glad I'm nearing the end.

Twenty-two minutes left. At this point, Bill Nye has become intolerable and I'm going out of my mind. I start to nose through the teacher's desk. She has a full box of Altoids in the top drawer, my flavor, too, but I'd never take one. I'd be pissed if somebody had their disgusting hands in my Altoids. *Altoids.* They're like the heroin of breath mints. Really, once you're into Altoids, you can't go back to Tic Tacs. No, Tic Tacs are just the gateway mint. Is that funny? Can I work that into a bit? Seventeen more minutes.

A girl with an adorable little outfit tiptoes into the classroom and hands me a note. I whisper, "Thank you," and smile sweetly because she looks so cute, and because now I have twelve minutes till freedom.

I unstaple the note. *What???*

"Please fill in for Mr. Thompson's eighth grade math honors class in room 312 during your prep Period Six."

No, no, there has to be a mistake! I have to go home to my ice cream! My Guiding Light! I'm sure one of the kids just saw me mouth, "Fuck!"

This is bullshit! I pout through the remaining moments of the stupid fucking video with nostrils flared, and realize I haven't been this riled up since the last time I saw Bastard Husband. The bell rings and I hurry out to find room 312.

Great. I have, like, three minutes to figure out what the fuck I'm supposed to do. The lesson plan…oh, no…this guy has to be kidding—no video? He actually expects me to teach? Well, there's no way in hell we're playing my three sentence game. No way. I'm not even putting my name on the board.

I don't know if it's because they're eighth graders or because they're honor students, but I have to admit these kids do seem a little more subdued. Except for this little asshole in the front row who hasn't shut his fucking mouth since the bell rang.

Keep it up, Asshole Boy. That's it, you little prick. Finally I walk over, point my finger in his face and bark, "Knock it awf!"

That felt good.

"Mr. Thomas left us a few problems to go over," I say.

"Thompson. It's Mr. Thompson," Asshole Boy corrects.

Does this kid have a death wish? I ignore him and fool with the focus on the overhead projector. "Okay, it says here, 'Matt's father is 45. He is 15 years older than twice Matt's age. How old is Matt?'" *Wait a minute—where's the answer key?* Oh, for Christsake.

I write "45" and "15" on the transparency and then stare at the two numbers. "Soooo… Who can tell the class what we do from here?"

One of the smart kids comes to my rescue. "I think it's 45 equals 2x…"

Asshole Boy interrupts. "You don't know how to find the answer, do you?"

Are you tawkin' to me? Stay calm, Ms. McNeil.

"As a matter of fact, I do know how to find the answer." I turn to the rest of the class. "You want to know how to find the answer?" I ask with the serenity of a monk. "You want to know how old Matt is?" I walk over to one of the boys. "You say, 'Hey, Matt—HOW OLD ARE YOU?' That's right, you JUST ASK HIM!"

I'm the Sam Kinison of substitute teachers. Super.

Was that a pin I heard drop? Even Asshole Boy is speechless. Surely the class appreciates such frank honesty; they probably don't get that much from adults.

A girl in a Mr. Bubble t-shirt breaks the silence. With dreamy eyes, she says, "You're the best sub we ever had."

My head nods in total agreement. "Well, sweetie, thank you. I appreciate that. But God willing, you'll never see me again."

I flip off the projector and offer one last nugget of wisdom. "Buy a calculator."

3.

The girl with the pierced face gazes into the air, fascinated by flakes of dust or whatever the hell she sees, obviously stoned out of her mind. The other one, I suspect, tied one on earlier in the day and now cradles her greasy head in her equally filthy hands as she succumbs to the inevitable hangover. I hate them both.

These aren't middle school kids. These two waste products are learning to become medical assistants, of all things. Two weeks ago I started working at one of those trade schools I mock for advertising during the Fox cartoon reruns. I'm supposed to be teaching a General Studies class—basic writing and math skills that even I don't need an answer key for. Only three students are on my roster; the good one, the only one who actually wants to learn, called in sick.

This is a part-time gig, from seven to eleven at night. I took it because I could still sub during the day, and more importantly, I'd still be able to look for a real job. And, of course, I need the money, especially now that I've had to pay for another background check, another set of fingerprints, and more copies of my official transcripts. Is there any job in Vegas that doesn't cost a fortune before you can start your first day of work?

The first couple of nights I earnestly tried to impart some knowledge, but quickly saw the futility of that. So here I sit, fantasizing about threading my pinkie through the ring protruding from Stony Girl's eyebrow and ripping it off her dopey face.

I don't feel the least bit guilty about my unkind and very unspiritual thoughts. The school is paying me fifteen dollars an hour to babysit these two, and they have the nerve to require a master's degree.

They can go fuck themselves. This is my last night.

§ § §

Mona has a two-for-one coupon for the cafe in Terrible's Casino, so we're catching up over their $8.95 prime rib. We haven't seen each other since before I left for Christmas, about two months ago. She's been in Israel, visiting her son who's studying to be a cantor, and up until last Friday, I was working evenings. Thank God that's over with.

"It's been so long! I want to hear everything," Mona says. "First, how do you like subbing?"

I roll my eyes. "I'm switching to high school. The middle school kids drive me nuts; they won't shut up."

"I know what you mean. The elementary grades are the same way." Her eyes brighten. "I interviewed for a fundraising job with the Agassi Foundation yesterday. Maybe something will happen with that and I'll get out of the schools."

"Yes," I say, crossing my fingers in the air. "Hopefully your luck will be better than mine. It's so discouraging. I've had so many interviews, and the only offers I get are for the shit jobs, like the one I just quit. Sure, they want me sell timeshares or graves, but the training position at the Hard Rock—the one job I really wanted—never came through. It's like dating; the one guy you really like never calls."

"Anything on the horizon?" she asks.

"Men or jobs?"

"Either."

"Nothing. I've had my eye on this comic at Boomers—his name is Perry—but of course, he hasn't been back in ages. What else? Oh, I responded to a posting to do freelance writing for a clinic that needed help with their website, and they actually called me back—which was a miracle—but then I find out it's a veterinary clinic."

Mona laughs in anticipation. She knows me.

"I told the woman, 'Look, I'm afraid of animals, but if you can keep them away from me and promise that no birds will fly into my head, I can do it, no problem.' Then she says no, no, I should love animals in order to write about them, and she'll find another writer. Can you imagine? Does she think I loved Six Sigma or gas turbines or any of the other crap I've written about? Animal people... they think I'm evil." I stab my steak. "Like I'm flushing kittens down the toilet in my spare time. I should have told her my rule."

"Your rule?"

I smile dementedly. "Any animal that wants to sniff my crotch has to buy me dinner first."

With that, Mona starts a fit of coughing and reaches for her water glass.

"Sorry, Mo," I say. "The boys at Boomers told me to dirty up my act, and since then my train of thought has been utterly disgusting."

"So I take it you didn't get the job."

"Duh. But enough of me. What's new with you?"

"Next Monday I start a job after school, three days a week. You'll love this: the Jewish princess is going to be a nanny for a Mexican family."

Now I reach for the water. "Jesus, Mona. You're a sitcom."

"What else can I do? If I don't make some money, I'm afraid I'll end up being a bag lady."

232

I've heard those exact words from two other women I know, and like Mona, their financial pictures were a lot more stable than mine. Mona's sitting on a house that will clear well over half a million after it's sold; I doubt she'll ever find herself camped beneath a highway overpass. I, on the other hand, have nearly depleted my savings and will soon be living off credit cards.

"I don't share the bag lady fear," I say. "Maybe I figure *somebody* will take me in, you know, as long as I keep working out." There's a shameful truth in that statement, which I'll examine some other time. "No, I'm afraid I'm not adequately releasing anger and resentment, and therefore all my pent-up emotions will manifest in my body as some horrible disease and I'll have no one to blame but myself."

Mona looks at me as if I'm crazy, but I can tell she wants to hear more, so I go on.

"It's all the New Age shit I read. I'm ready to throw my whole spiritual library out the fucking window. Sometimes I'm busting with anger and then I think oh, no, I shouldn't feel this way—Bijan says everything is perfect, Louise Hay says resentment gives you cancer." Deep breath. "I ask myself, why can't I find a decent job? Am I not manifesting hard enough? Or is it because I allow myself to think negative thoughts, so that's all I can attract into my life? I feel like I'm playing the game the best I can, and I'm still failing miserably.

"For two weeks I subbed starting at seven thirty in the morning and then taught that other stupid fucking class until eleven at night. For all that, I made a hundred and fifty dollars a day, *one-third* of what I made back east. Meanwhile, he's still the highest paid professor in the university—this divorce hasn't affected *him* financially—*and* he has the nerve to send me emails bragging about his gambling winnings. I can hardly pay my cable bill, but I'm not supposed to feel resentful. So if I ever get cancer, just so you know, Mona, it'll be my own fault." Dammit, I don't want to cry in the restaurant.

My friend nods in agreement at all the appropriate places. God bless her for letting me rant as I do. "I'm going to start babysitting in the hotels," she says. "Ten dollars an hour, plus tips. I registered with a service. They're waiting for the results of my background check. Do you want me to give you their number?"

"No. But thank you." I notice my chest heaving. "Jesus, Mona, doesn't it piss you off that you have to work three jobs? I'm, like, so fucking pissed. He has money to gamble and I'm wondering if I should downsize to a one-bedroom apartment when, by the way, I used to have a three bedroom house, which, by the way, I sold and commingled the funds like an idiot because gee, I thought my marriage was going to last a lot longer than two and a half lousy fucking years."

The waiter heard the last of that one. Mona grabs the check from his hand.

"Do you want to be in a focus group?" she asks, fumbling through her purse. "This market research company pays you anywhere from fifty dollars on up just for your opinion. I do it all the time. They asked me if I knew anyone."

Now *that* I'll consider, especially since I hold my opinions in such high esteem. "Sure. What do I do?"

"You look at different products and tell them what you think. I'll give them your number. They'll call and ask a bunch of questions to see if you qualify, so sometimes you have to lie."

"I don't know if I can lie," I say, my spiritual bent apparently on the rebound.

"No, it's okay—you have to lie or they won't put you in the group. Last week they paid me sixty-five dollars to look at adult diapers. They asked if I had an incontinence problem and I had to say, 'yes' or they wouldn't have used me."

I shudder. "Oh, Mona…Think of the karma."

"Hey, it's sixty-five dollars. It's easier to lie about wearing Depends than try to get money out of Alan." Mona has that throw-up burp face whenever she talks about him. "And what about your ex? Besides his gambling winnings, anything new?"

"I got an email from him yesterday," I say. The tears I put on hold earlier now descend. "He's going back to New Zealand at the end of the semester. This time for good."

4.

Grandpa Simpson stops at my barstool and shouts, "Why don't you give me your phone number?"

I turn around, expecting to find an elderly lady somewhere behind me, but unfortunately that's not the case. His question is directed at me.

"Give me your number!" he demands.

I fervently shake my head, bewildered that I'm now attracting men twice my mother's age. Grandpa stands for a moment looking through me, not at me, as if he's wondering whether he left the house with the iron on, then shuffles away without another word.

The pub in the Orleans Casino has become one of my favorite places to plant myself. Earlier I did a set at some little bar I'd never been to out on West Sahara. One of the comics from Boomers is trying to get a stage going there and he asked me to do fifteen minutes—a long time for me, but still far from an HBO special.

The night ended in time for me to catch some music, and not one to waste a cute little slutty-blouse outfit, I came over here to unwind. Looks like the band is just about done with their break; one by one they reassemble and strap on their guitars. I position my seat, as I like to do, with my back against the bar to get the best view of the stage.

A tattooed biker type with a goatee and shaved head keeps glancing my way from the other side of the L-shaped bar, and from where I sit, I'll be damned if he doesn't look like a cross between Billy Bob Thornton and Charlie Manson. Sure enough, with drink in one hand and cigarette in the other, Slingblade heads over and takes the barstool next to mine. I keep my eyes on the performers. Dazed octogenarians and crazed serial killers—what kind of message am I sending out tonight to attract these nuts? Oh, it's probably the comedy boobs.

I feel his eyes beaming into me, and can tell he's itching to converse. Shit. I really just want to sit here and chill by myself. Thankfully, the music starts up. I send a flirty smile to the bass player, pretending he's my boyfriend. Yes, I'm with the band.

"Have you seen theses guys before?" Slingblade asks. His gravelly voice matches his appearance.

I nod in his direction, avoiding eye contact, but I bet if I looked at him straight-on, there'd be a swastika etched in his forehead. I sip my beer.

"My name's Paul. Do you want to dance?"

"No, I don't dance," I answer in his direction. "But thank you." I maintain my focus. Although he keeps himself at a respectable physical distance, on a cosmic level his energy is all over me, totally invading my space.

"Baby, why won't you dance with me?" he asks. I glance down toward the floor as he speaks. Nice shoes.

Finally I turn to face him. "Because you look like a murderer," I answer politely. But as the words leave my mouth, I realize that's not quite the case. He's more handsome, his eyes much kinder than I expected. There's an intensity about him, to be sure, but I also detect a vulnerability. I soften a bit myself and teasingly ask, "Well, *have* you ever killed someone?"

"Yes," he replies, as simply as if my question were, "Is today Wednesday?" I don't quite know what to make of his response. He holds his cocktail with his pinkie in the air, like my friend Chief. I'm sure that's not the killer's way of drinking.

"I do stand-up," I tell him. "I did a set before I came here. The boobs are part of my comedy persona. Just so you know, I'm not a hooker."

"I didn't think you were," he assures me. He has a nice smile.

The band begins to play a slow, reggae version of "Knockin' on Heaven's Door" that blends perfectly with the buzz I'm starting to feel from my second Guinness. Despite my proximity to an admitted killer, I'm digging the scene; I don't get to hear much music like this in Vegas and I'm not afraid of a stinkin' murderer.

He puts out his cigarette and sets his drink on the bar. "Come on, let's dance" he says, patting my arm.

Ordinarily I'd shoot a scathing glare to anyone who'd dare to touch my arm without my permission. Instead, the voice in my head says, *Go ahead, give him a chance. He's harmless.*

Oh, so he's a *harmless* killer. They're the best kind.

I hesitate, pointing to the empty floor in front of the band. "No, no one else is dancing."

"We'll dance right here." He moves a couple of tables in front of our barstools to create our private dance floor, then takes my hand. "Come on."

We seem to move well together, or maybe it's the alcohol. At any rate, I don't have to think about the dance steps, which leaves my mind open for other thoughts. It's been almost a year since I've been this close to a man, and God knows when I last slow-danced with anyone. Slingblade holds me tight, but doesn't try to grind himself into me or slide his hands down my ass as I might have feared. His tight little body is not much bigger than mine. It's nice. He must work out.

"Are you married?" he asks in my ear.

"No." I don't tell him I took my ring off only yesterday. "You?"

"Married thirty-five years. Separated three months."

Thirty-five years. Yikes. Unless he got married when he was three, he's way too old for me. Whatever—we're only dancing.

The band must be playing the extended, "In-a-Gadda-da-Vida" version of Dylan's song. I feel we've been holding onto each other for twenty minutes or so. I could go another twenty; I'm into it. His shirt is soft, good quality. He doesn't dress like a killer. I don't even think he's a biker. *Paul.* That's not a killer's name. Isn't that a saint?

It's good to dance. I feel sexy. Funny—I like to dress sexy all the time, but I never actually feel sexy. This was a good idea. I'm glad I listened to the voice in my head. Maybe for once it really was the voice of reason.

We sit out only a song or two. The band finishes the night with an Aiko-Aiko/Jambalaya medley that reminds me of the many JazzFests I've been to in New Orleans. This was so much fun. We linger as the band packs their instruments, then walk out together through the casino floor.

We stop when I point to an exit beyond the rows of slots. "I'm parked this way."

"I'm over there," he says. "Baby, why don't you give me your number? I want to take you out Saturday night."

Without a thought, I give him one of the business cards I've been distributing at those stupid networking meetings.

He looks it over. "Technical writer. I hope you don't have to work tomorrow."

"No. Actually I'm still looking for a writing job. In the meantime I'm subbing in the school district," I say, with the obligatory roll of the eyes. "I'll take the phone off the hook when I get home so they don't call me at freakin' six o'clock in the morning." That's about four hours from now. "How about you?" I ask. "What do you do?"

"Nothing."

"Nothing? You have to do *something.*"

"I'm retired."

"Retired?" I didn't expect to hear "retired." A work release program, yes. I'll flatter him anyway. "Aren't you a little young?"

"Well... I'm on a hundred percent disability."

Hold on—weren't we dancing for the past hour and a half?

He pulls at the dog tags dangling around his neck. "'Nam."

"Oh." I scan his body and wave my finger toward his crotch. "Does everything... um... work?"

"Yeah," he laughs, and then adds, "It's a mental disability."

"Whew!" I giggle and wipe imaginary sweat from my forehead. "Thank God, huh?" Hold on—sirens and flashing lights. "Wait... What does that mean?"

"I have PTSD. Post-traumatic stress disorder."

"Post-traumatic stress disorder? Men don't usually get that until *after* they've been with me a while." *Jesus Linda, does everything have to be a joke?* "I'm sorry."

He waves off my stupid humor. "I'm still all fucked up. I'm working on it, though. The VA has support groups. I go to a couple of them. My psychiatrist says I'm doing well. He thinks he's got me on the right meds now."

Psychiatrist? Meds?

"I don't mean to scare you off," he says, evidently reading the concern on my face. "but I have to be honest with you."

I nod.

"You still want to go out with me Saturday night?"

"Did you kill anyone outside of Vietnam?"

"No." He smiles. "I've wanted to, I'm not gonna lie about that."

"We've all wanted to," I say. "Okay, then."

"Good. I'll talk to you before the weekend." He hugs me good-bye and I head to my car.

Psychiatrist. I can only conclude that my guardian angels hate me. They're supposed to be on my side, but no, I imagine them doubled over, convulsing with laughter, having pulled a good one over me this time. How many men—and women—have asked me to dance in the past ten months? And how many have times have I said "yes"? Once. Why? Because my brilliant intuition told me to go ahead, give this guy a chance. And they let me do it. They're assholes; my guardian angels are a bunch of assholes. First they send me this fucked-up Kiwi "soulmate" and now they let me give my phone number to a complete whack job.

I put the key in the ignition.

Oooh…I hope he calls.

§ § §

Paul followed through and picked me up Saturday night promptly at eight o'clock. "Here, baby. I brought you something," he said, handing me a pamphlet entitled Understanding PTSD.

It's no doubt some kind of warning signal when your date arrives at your door not with flowers in hand, but a brochure detailing his chronic mental disorder. In retrospect, I suppose the gesture was rather considerate; I might have been spared untold turmoil had Bastard Husband entered my life with the appropriate paperwork. To be fair, I could have reciprocated with a handout of my own entitled What You Should Know About Incessant Nagging.

In the past two months, I've become a veritable subject matter expert on Post-Traumatic Stress Disorder, something I never aspired to, though I certainly never imagined I'd be an authority on addictive behavior, either. So now I'm perusing the Internet with a whole new research project, the disturbing list of my "recently viewed items" on Amazon proof of my innate ability to sniff out troubled men.

Mona simply shook her head when I told her about Paul. In my defense I contended the attraction was there before I knew a thing about his PTSD, but she says the shaved head and tattoos should have been enough of a tip-off that something was wrong. I hate to think I harbor a creepy self-serving need to play the rescuer role, and prefer to believe that people come into our lives because they're exactly who we need to be with in this present moment. Though the argument could be made—isn't it about time someone normal crossed my path?

Paul is definitely not normal. Anyone who admits to starting a road rage incident in the parking lot after his anger management class is not normal. Anyone who starts a fistfight with his boss and then, upon getting fired, walks into another business in the same strip mall, all bloodied and disheveled, and applies for another job is not normal, either. What's even less normal, however, is the fact that he actually was hired. Paul's had thirty-four employers in thirty-four years, he told me. People with PTSD have authority issues, and therefore have trouble holding jobs. Just ask me, I'm an expert on the topic.

I've never been around anyone whose life has been haunted by war. During the Vietnam era, I was young and absorbed in issues of importance like impressing boyfriends and scoring a fake ID. Sure, I saw snippets of the carnage during the six o'clock news—we weren't bombarded round the clock by cable broadcasts back then—but that was the extent of my exposure. I had no relatives called to war, no friends who lost older brothers serving their country.

For me, Vietnam produced an era of great music, and I remember wishing I were a few years older, to be part of the Woodstock generation and participate in the sit-ins and love-ins and anti-war protests. The closest I came was in 1980, when I left the babies with Chris and took a bus with some girlfriends to Washington, D.C. to attend a No Nukes rally. As someone who's never been able to grasp the concepts of atoms and molecules, nuclear anything was way beyond my level of comprehension, but Jackson Browne was associated with the cause and he was cute as hell. Though we tried to catch the wave of spirited dissent, the scene was nothing but a party and now I have to live the rest of my life knowing I protested against kind old Jimmy Carter, probably the most peace-minded president we've ever had.

For the most part, Paul seems perfectly normal, especially given my last point of reference, though some of the PTSD behavior takes some getting used to. I found out the hard way not to trigger his startle response; I now cough or clear my throat when approaching him from behind. And reports of the day's casualties in Iraq often prompt him to hole himself up with the blinds closed, sometimes for days. "I get in a bad way," he explains, "so if you don't hear from me, don't worry, it has nothing to do with you. I'll call you when I come out the other side."

I appreciate his efforts to protect me from the crossfire—when Bastard Husband's clouds darkened, he'd storm all over me with gale force winds—and I respect Paul for having the courage to explore his dark interior. He attends his support groups and is willing to confront the enemy, though now the enemy's within. I admire him for being self-aware and open to self-exploration. Not everyone is.

A few weeks ago I mailed my dog-eared copy of *The Addictive Mind* to my stormy ex, figuring it would serve him better than me. Lesson learned: Don't expect people to thank you for sending them self-help books, even when you've thoughtfully highlighted the parts that specifically pertain to them. I guess that's like placing a can of deodorant in the smelly girl's locker at school. He did acknowledge my good intentions—with an email explaining the uselessness of books like that and that it's possible to overanalyze a horse race.

At any rate, Paul's been a blast to hang out with and we enjoy quite the party life together. I used to avoid the Strip, but now I embrace Las Vegas Boulevard in all its neon glory, maybe because for once, someone else is driving.

"Mr. Vegas," as he likes to call himself, is well connected in town—everyone he knows seems willing to comp us in exchange for a few bucks passed in a handshake. We dine in four-star restaurants and get the best tables at the comedy and variety shows he takes me to. Sometimes we go to the locals' places, where Paul knows which bartenders will barter free drinks in exchange for the Viagra or antidepressants he can get from the VA.

Paul's son, who's also his best friend, manages one of the ultralounges on the Strip and makes sure we're well taken care of. The bouncer unhooks the velvet ropes just for us as we bypass the line and then cozy up on the cushiony sofas reserved for the bottle service patrons. Doting waitresses, who now know me by name, serve complimentary cocktails or come over just to say hi or show off a new boob job. I try to picture myself in their scanty outfits, and think I could probably pull it off if I lost a few pounds. Who cares that I'm comparing myself to women literally half my age? It's best to keep your standards high. The good news is, I've accelerated my workout regimen considerably as a result of being around these seductive young chickies.

Even though Paul's ten years older than me, his body is strong and fit, and with all the scars and tattoos, he's an anatomical museum. There's the portrait of his hero, Che Guevara, inked over his right pectorals, a Buddha good luck symbol on his back, a serpent climbing up his neck, and many detailed images of war—a skeleton in a Marine's uniform, a soldier being shot in the back, a graveyard with one tombstone etched with a fallen comrade's dying words, "Help me." The scenes so embedded into his psyche seem to emerge through his skin.

And then there are the scars—the bullet wounds that earned him his two Purple Hearts, the thin, vertical line running down his chest from quadruple bypass surgery, evidence of mental stress taking its physical toll. So much to scrutinize on that little body of his, and like museum artifacts, you don't really know what you're looking at until you've heard the stories behind them.

"What's this one from?" I asked late one night as I rubbed my finger over a little crater in his back.

"Shrapnel," he replied, then went into a war story, as he often does when we lie together. This time he told of his platoon rushing through a rice paddy amid mortar explosions and flying debris.

"A bullet ripped though my sergeant's jaw, like in slow motion," he said. "I can still see the blood in his beard…bullets zooming past our heads, people falling and screaming, 'I'm hit!'" He re-enacted the battle as if it happened last week. "Then an explosion went off and I went down. They took me to a hooch where they kept the wounded. Because my wounds were minor, they let me help out the corpsmen. All I did was hold the other Marines' hands, trying to comfort them as they died. A lot of boys were calling for their mothers."

Paul closed his eyes. All his bedtime stories end the same way.

"Why did I live and they didn't?" he asked.

I never know what to say. What is the proper response?

Paul's narrations moved me to write a poem, the first I'd ever attempted.

For Paul

My heart aches
to hear the horrors of his past,
the grieving for an ambushed youth.

He remains armed;
the struggle continues within.

I am careful not to intrude, and
offer only the comfort of the present
while I whisper, "Triumph is certain"
for I can see

His heart still loves.

I don't know if it's any good or not, but his eyes welled when I gave it to him and a week later he showed up with another a tattoo. "Ambushed Youth," it says.

Paul and I have fun together, with no sense of obligation. We both know he's too crazy to have any kind of normal relationship, so we just enjoy each other, realizing "it is what it is." Some people are easier to appreciate from the periphery rather than the epicenter.

5.

The phone rings as the credits roll on *Guiding Light*. It must be Paul. He knows to wait until three o'clock when my soap is over.

"Hello?" I coo into the receiver.

"Is this Linda?"

"Yes." I don't recognize the voice.

"You don't know me. I'm a friend of your husband's."

My *husband*? I don't have a stinkin' husband.

"I…I don't know how to tell you this…" the man says.

Last fall's drive to the emergency room flashes into my brain, as well as the accompanying sense of dread. "What is it?" I ask, bracing myself.

"He's missing."

"Missing?" That could mean anything. "For how long?"

"Since one-thirty this morning. That's when I left him at the Crown and Anchor."

"The Crown and Anchor? That bar on Tropicana?" I pause to process what I'm hearing. Wait…"I'm sorry…Who am I speaking with?"

The caller tells me his name is Don and I place him right away. He's a retired guy Bastard Husband befriended in the race and sports book in Green Valley Ranch. I've heard his name mentioned many times.

"Your husband's been staying at my house," Don says, "until he leaves for New Zealand next Monday."

Monday is May 31, a year to the day since his last trip. Only this time there's no ambiguity surrounding his return. That reality presses on my heart.

"I couldn't get him to go home with me," Don explains. "He said he'd take a cab, but never showed up. I found his cell phone here on my kitchen table. That's how I got your number." He sighs. "I'm sick over this. I don't know what to do. I called the police and checked with the hospitals—nothing."

Police? Hospitals? Poor old Don's a novice at dealing with this type of bullshit. You call the cops and check the morgues when a normal person disappears.

"Don't worry," I say. "This happens all the time. It's been only what? Fifteen hours? He'll turn up." Yeah, call me back if he hasn't surfaced by next week.

"Well, this is a little inconsiderate of him, don't you think?" Don's exasperation is precious.

I suppress a sarcastic retort. "Yes, he's being very inconsiderate." Common courtesy—Bastard Husband has yet to master that one.

Before we hang up, I add, "Call me when you hear from him, will you?"

§ § §

Twenty after eight. No word.

The lights of the valley start to twinkle in the dusk. I stand at my window wondering where he is and whether he's safe, as I've done so many times. He's vulnerable right now—shit hits the fan whenever anything finishes for him. The semester ended a couple of weeks ago, and now a fourteen-year period of living in the U.S. is coming to a close as well. He's ripe for a blowout of mega proportions.

I call his cell phone. After five or six rings, it goes to voice mail. I don't leave a message.

My mind plays its Greatest Hits of Morbid Scenarios, each one ending with him lying dead somewhere and no one can identify the body. Lovely. It's been a while since I tormented my brain like this, but the truth is, when you're blind drunk from ingesting a million beers, sooner or later your luck runs out. And he seems to enjoy the reckless thrill of taunting fate. It's a miracle nothing horrible has happened to him, at least nothing I know of. Nothing yet. God's been keeping a close eye on that one, like the incorrigible schoolboy in the desk pushed next to the teacher's.

Where the hell is he?

I just talked to him last Wednesday night. We've spoken a few times over the past several months, all cordial, but distant, exchanges. I'm the one who always calls him; we've had one lingering retirement fund issue to settle per our divorce agreement. Although the situation could certainly be handled by email, I'd rather talk to him so I can better gauge his state of mind and well-being. Despite my "Let go and let God" mantra, I'm compelled to check now and then to make sure God is, in fact, staying on top of things.

Last week, however, B.H. called *me*, and we had a very pleasant chat. He mentioned he's looking forward to teaching at his alma mater, and for once the conversation wasn't dominated by detailed accounts of his stupid horse betting. I think he even asked me a question—I forget about what.

At one point he launched into his famous impression of Ozzy Osbourne, "the great philosopher," as he calls him. As always, I laughed hard as he mumbled away like the befuddled rocker, and I reminded him how he used to cry, "Shar-ron!" when he needed me to find something that inevitably was right in front of him. We loved watching *The Osbournes*. I'd marvel at his ability to translate Ozzy's unintelligible mutterings and then reciprocate when he couldn't understand a word of *Bernie Mac*.

I enjoyed having a laugh as we did, especially after such a long time, though the mere whiff of his good side made me long for the person I fell in love with back in Niagara Falls and continued to adore during our adventures in Wyoming and Utah. Before we hung up that night, he said, "I'm sorry about everything, eh." Although part of me wanted to scoff at his admission, I accepted his apology and said I was sorry for any anguish I'd caused him during our time together.

Time supposedly does us a favor by fading the bad memories from our mental landscapes and preserving the pleasant ones, though in his case, it would be less painful if the ugliness could remain in the forefront. I don't miss him when I think he's an asshole. Sometimes there's a hellish road laid out before you and love tricks you into thinking it's all worth it.

Where *is* he?

Was our last conversation so enjoyable because he wanted to end things with me amiably? Or did he subconsciously know that would be the last we'd ever speak? I think of drugged-up hospice patients who come back to life and have a lucid conversation right before they die. Super—a new morbid thought to add to the collection. Jesus, I'm freakin' mental.

At nine-thirty the phone rings. It's Don. There is now an official missing person's report, number 040512-1911. He relays the contact information from the police department; my hand shakes as I write.

I thank Don for his efforts, and again ask him to keep me posted. "Don't worry, he'll walk through your door any minute," I try to assure him. He'll be totally oblivious to the chaos he's caused and you'll want to kick his fucking ass.

No sooner do we hang up and the phone rings again. "You were right," Don says. "He just walked in. I'm glad he's okay, but I could kill him."

Really? Get in line.

§ § §

The back room at Boomers is nearly empty, maybe because of the holiday weekend. I notice only a handful of lay people in the audience. I'm glad I'm not going up tonight—there's nothing worse than performing for a roomful of comics. Not only have they heard your act a hundred times already, comics never laugh. I find a seat in the back and say hi to Danny Wilborne, Shuli, and Smelly Dick Boy, who offers a big Italian Stallion hug.

The guys are sweet to me, and even though most of them are my kids' age, they never make me feel like an old bat. Well, maybe once, when Danny said I reminded him of the Sally Field character in the movie *Punchline*. I took that as anything but a compliment, and wondered how I could possibly resemble a frumpy housewife when I'm sporting such an awesome Vegas rack.

Joe Lowers is back in town; he's been on the road for the past few weeks, and it's good to see him. I adore that guy.

"Linda Lou, you going up tonight?" he asks.

I shake my head. "I've been working on some new stuff, but it's not together yet. I need a couple of weeks."

"Hey, Jenny and I are having a barbecue tomorrow. Two o'clock. A bunch of comics will be stopping by. You have any plans?"

"Plans? As if."

"Here, call me in the morning for directions to the house." Joe hands me a business card with a picture of him on stage dancing in his shorts and bowling shirt.

I can't help but smile. "You're such a goof."

I watch Joe make the rounds before the show starts. As the lights dim, my Guinness goes down the wrong pipe and while I'm hacking away, who sits next to me but my crush-of-all-crushes, Perry.

"Hey, Linda Lou. You all right?"

"Yeah," I squeak, trying to regain composure between involuntary gulps. I hold up my glass. "I have a drinking problem."

Perry says he wishes I were performing tonight and then rises, I assume for a trip out to the bar. Marcus starts his warm-up-the-crowd routine, and after the second comic takes the stage, Perry still hasn't come back. Damn. It's an off night; I bet he left.

The energy in the room is noticeably low and the comics seem to half-heartedly go through their sets. Now and then I catch my mind wandering, and every time it roams into Bastard Husband territory, especially the fact that he's leaving tomorrow, I redirect my focus to more pleasant thoughts, like Perry's coolness. I wish I knew how old he is. It's hard to tell; I hope he's around forty. But he's probably not forty. He looks young, like one of those people who never change. He could be twenty-five for all I know.

How young can I go and still have a conscience? And why the hell isn't he back here sitting next to me?

Before I know it the show is over and the lights come up. Quick sets tonight; no one was really into it. We all seem to bolt away, except the comics who linger at the banquette waiting to sign up for future stage time.

"I'll give you a buzz in the morning," I tell Joe Lowers, with a playful poke. On my way to the door, I notice Perry at the bar talking to some guy I don't recognize.

He sees me and waves me over. "Linda Lou!"

I sashay to their barstools like the oversexed hospice volunteer that I am.

"Benny, this is Linda," he says.

I offer my hand, my desire to appear gracious eclipsing my stupid germ phobia. Benny smiles and nods.

"Linda's really funny," my crush tells his friend. "You'll have to see her set."

Perry thinks I'm funny.

He sips the last of the melting ice in his glass. "Hey, the stage at Norma Jean's starts at eleven. We're going over—want to come?"

Benny interrupts before I can answer. "I can't go. I gotta head home," he says, in a growl suggesting a proclivity for Camel Filters. "You two go ahead."

Perry looks at me. "You up for it?"

"Sure!" I whoop. Is Marcia Brady up for Davy Jones? This is perfect. I don't have to sub tomorrow because of the holiday, so I can stay out all night if I want.

Perry tells me we're going just a few blocks away and why don't I follow him. During the short drive, I notice he has a Saturn, too, though his is a later model. Good thing I settled on this little beaded camisole and denim miniskirt combo after all. I was afraid my cute outfit would go to waste tonight.

The stage at Norma Jean's is up by the front window, right in the main bar area. That's a tough setup—the comics have to compete with the televisions above the bar and the din from the people who came to sit and talk. That's why I like Boomers. Even though it's a dive, at least everyone in the back room is there to watch the show.

Conditions are rarely favorable for performing comedy, so I'm learning. You need enough people in the crowd (who aren't comics themselves), a decent sound system, no peripheral distractions... and on top of all that, my requirements include a good hair day, a cute outfit, an effective pre-performance meditation, and perfect planetary alignment. The chances of all that coming together are pretty damn slim. Comedy is much harder than I ever imagined, and it doesn't seem to get any easier.

Looks like it'll be a while before anything happens on this stage. In the Vegas open mic world, an eleven o'clock show time means midnight, if you're lucky. What do I care? I'm with Perry. I can stay out all freakin' night.

We have no problem finding two barstools together. "What would you like, sweetheart?" he asks, and then orders a Newcastle for me and a Diet Coke for himself.

I realize I've never seen him with anything but soda. "You don't drink, do you?"

"No, not in years. I used to," he says, then with a mischievous grin adds, "It's best that I don't. Crazy days of youth."

I point to my pint. "Do you mind if I…"

"Oh, no. All my friends drink. No, please."

That's awesome. Though a guy with a wild streak is a definite turn-on, I'm just as happy to hear those days are over for him.

"So you have a Saturn, too," I comment. "They're great cars, huh? I just hit a hundred and forty thousand miles." My tone implies he should seethe with jealousy. "I've had it almost nine years and it's never let me down." I raise my glass. "Now there's a successful long-term relationship."

I don't know if Perry is laughing at me or with me, but he's laughing, and that's a good sign. I feel comfortable with him, and even though I rattle away, being my total idiot self, I get the feeling he nonetheless finds me witty and charming.

As we talk, I can tell I have Perry's full attention and I love, love, *love* the fact that he never once glances up at the TV. When I'm with a guy, I want "all eyes on Linda," and if someone would rather stare at a baseball game or a goddamn Viagra commercial than enjoy my beautification efforts, there's something horribly wrong. The best part is he asks me questions—how old are my kids, how long have I been watching *Guiding Light*—what a treat. The men I'm used to are as self-absorbed as I am. Paul can't escape from Vietnam, and Bastard Husband...

Is leaving tomorrow.

Stop. This is Perry time.

I'm able to refocus without effort. Perry is so freakin' cool. I dig his looks and this jewelry thing he has going on intrigues me—the silver earring peeking from under his hair, the heavy chain hanging from his wrist, the thin leather strap around his neck. I don't want to stare, but I think I counted three rings on each hand, including one on his right thumb. I'm sure I've never known a guy with a thumb ring. I have some questions of my own for this hipster on the barstool next to me.

"So, what do you do?" I ask. "You know, for work."

Perry tells me he's a waiter at one of the trendy restaurants that, according to the gossip columnist in the newspaper, is one of the best places for celebrity sightings. I'm dying to know who he's served, being the tabloid addict that I am, but instead play it cool and ask where he's from.

"Dallas," is the answer.

"Dallas? Where's your accent? You must have left Texas a long time ago."

"Ten years," he says. "I came to Las Vegas right after I turned thirty."

"So you're forty?" Brilliant, Linda—did you work that out yourself? *He's forty.*

"Yeah, I'll be forty-one in October."

"Really? October what?"

"Tenth."

"So you're a Libra, too. My birthday's on the third." We're both Libras and we both drive Saturns. Cosmic.

The bartender places another round of drinks in front of us. I pull out my wallet, but Perry will have no part of that. Just as well; I'm not sure how much I actually have in there. By now the show has begun, and not wanting to be like the annoying people who talk through the performers' sets, we politely direct our attention to the stage, whispering commentary now and then. The host looks like an old pothead whose face has frozen into a squinty-eyed, buzzed expression. He rambles on while we wait for a punch line that never materializes and he gives the comics way too much time, especially the ones who are drunk and have no decipherable act. I'm annoyed to see them fucking around like that. Marcus does a good job running the stage at Boomers. I don't like Stony Dude's stinkin' looks.

Perry and I hang out until the last comic finishes his set, and by now it's well after two.

"I should get going before I start to wilt," I say. Like Cinderella, I want to make a getaway while I'm still looking good. Perry walks me to my car and after I thank him for the beers, he gives me a warm hug. Beneath his Roger Waters t-shirt, there's a little bit of a belly to sink into. I like that.

Cruising south on the 15, I mentally replay snippets of the evening's conversation, and have a little debate with myself as to whether or not Perry has tattoos, and does he wear all that jewelry to bed? I vote "no" on the body ink, and conclude that he does, in fact, sleep fully bedecked in silver, though the leather choker lies on the nightstand. As my mind wanders to the fun we could have in the playground between the sheets, my car steers itself off the Tropicana exit ramp with an inexplicable sense of urgency.

I pull into the parking lot at the Crown and Anchor.

It's Bastard Husband's last night in this country. He was drinking here a few days ago; maybe he's come back for one last binge. I hurry toward the entrance. Tomorrow he leaves for the other side of the world. I may never see him again. He has to be here.

Sweeping through the bar, I scan the bodies of the Sunday night patrons in various states of intoxication, and although a beefy fellow with a cigarette in one hand and a pint in the other catches my eye, the glazed smirk belongs to someone else.

He's not here.

I may never see him again.

6.

"It's like a death, eh," he said the last time we spoke, referring to the end of our relationship. I bit my tongue. More like a suicide. Preventable, if you ask me.

He's gone. Fuck.

It's just as well that he wasn't at the Crown and Anchor last night. Seeing him, being in his physical presence again, would have made this moment even more painful. I think of hospice patients and how at the end loved ones hold on for dear life—literally—when it's in everyone's best interest to let go and allow the person to transition to the next leg of the journey.

In the end, our hearts beat only for ourselves. And unlike my hospice patients, his heart still beats—he's *not* dead, for Christsake—so who knows, maybe I *will* see him again someday. And maybe at that point the lines of communication will be free from the static of our individual fears.

"Dismantling a relationship is an act of love," says one of my spiritual books. I like to believe that on some level he knew the path he had to walk was wide enough only for one, and his pushing me away was, in fact, an act of kindness. I'll never know if that's true; it's what I like to think.

I sit here on my couch, wrapped in a post-mortem sense of peace that seems to dam the tears.

During his lecture last Friday, Bijan defined peace as "the lack of resistance," and said as soon as we resist the natural course of the universe, we move away from peace and into turmoil. Looking back at this past year, I realize I could have saved myself untold turmoil had I not resisted so much, had I not been so goddamn hell-bent on jamming the square peg into the round hole, had I accepted the simple fact that—guess what?—people don't always act the way you want them to.

You can't have an agenda for someone, can you? We set our expectations in concrete and conclude that life will positively suck if things don't materialize exactly as we envision. I think that's the problem with marriage—we go into it presuming we'll live happily ever after and as soon as the person endangers the dream, we freak out. When we insist events unfold a certain way, everything gets fucked up. That's what Deepak Chopra says. Not in those exact words.

I could deliver a five-hour discourse on lessons learned, but I will give myself credit for doing some things right. I knew enough to reach out for the help available to me, to join the divorce support group and sample all those nutty spiritual churches. I'm glad I pressed myself to go out and explore the town all alone, and that I had the balls to try stand-up comedy. That reminds me, I have to call Joe Lowers for directions to his house.

I am going to a cook-out today with my comic friends.

I have comic friends!

Perry is a comic friend. Oh, the thought of him brings me joy. Mona says the sparkle's in my eye whenever I mention his name.

"So, do you think you two will get together?" she's asked more than once.

My answer is, "I have no idea." For all I know, he may have a girlfriend—I wasn't going to ask last night—or maybe he's not even into me, in that way. Maybe he's just a nice guy befriending an aging nymph trying to regain her footing. The truth is, I may never see *him* again, either, and if that's the case, well, that would suck, but so be it. He would always be Perfect Perry in the Jesus halo and I'll never know whether or not he has tattoos or sleeps in his jewelry. And he'll never know about the nasty stretch marks on my stomach or the cellulite that's been congregating on my ass.

So whatever happens or doesn't happen with Perry will be perfect. Everything will unfold in divine order just as…just as it did with Bastard Husband.

I can't help but smile. Our three years together were like one of those carnival rides that makes you scream your head off in both terror and exhilaration, then when you're finally on solid ground, you puke your guts out and swear you'll never do that again. But once the heaving stops, you realize that was the most exciting thing you've ever done, the most fun you've ever had.

And you're back in line, buying another ticket.

About the Author

Las Vegas-based Linda Lou is a humor writer, spirited blogger and occasional stand-up comic. Her essays have been published in a number of anthologies including *Chicken Soup for the Soul: Divorce and Recovery*. She speaks frequently about writing, the creative process and topics related to the empowerment of women over 40. Contact Linda at linda@bastardhusband.com.

Breinigsville, PA USA
12 March 2010
234093BV00001B/3/P